CATHOLIC DEVOTIONS

Litanies of the Catholic Church

Compiled from Traditional Sources, with an Introduction

Copyright © 2021 by Catholic Devotions

All rights reserved. No part of this publication may be reproduced, stored or transmitted in any form or by any means, electronic, mechanical, photocopying, recording, scanning, or otherwise without written permission from the publisher. It is illegal to copy this book, post it to a website, or distribute it by any other means without permission.

First edition

This book was professionally typeset on Reedsy.
Find out more at reedsy.com

Contents

Introduction vi
How to Use Litanies in Prayer vi

I   Official Litanies of the Church

Litany of the Holy Name of Jesus 3
Litany of the Sacred Heart 7
Litany of the Blessed Virgin Mary (Litany of Loreto) 10
Litany of the Saints 14
Litany of St. Joseph 20

II   Litanies to the Persons of the Holy Trinity

Litany of the Most Holy Trinity 27
Litany of the Incarnate Word 31
Litany of the Infant Jesus 35
Litany of the Life of Jesus Christ 40
Litany of the Passion 43
Litany of the Resurrection 48
Litany of Jesus Glorified 52
Litany of the Precious Blood of the Sacred Heart of Jesus 56
Litanies of the Sacred Heart of Jesus for Every Day of the... 59
   MONDAY: Litany of the Sacred Heart of the Child Jesus 59
   TUESDAY: Litany of the Sacred Heart of Jesus Conversing Amongst Men 61

WEDNESDAY: Litany of the Sacred Heart of Jesus Dwelling in Solitude	63
THURSDAY: Litany of the Sacred Heart of Jesus in the Blessed Sacrament	65
FRIDAY: Litany of the Sacred Heart of Jesus Suffering	67
SATURDAY: Litany of the Sacred Heart of Jesus Dying	69
SUNDAY: Litany of the Sacred Heart of Jesus Risen from the Dead	71
Litany in Honor of the Holy Ghost	73
Litany of the Holy Ghost for Pentecost	77
Litany of the Love of God	81
Litany of Glory	84

III   Litanies to the Blessed Virgin Mary

Litany of the Dolors of the Blessed Virgin Mary	91
Litany of the Holy Name of Mary	95
Litany of the Immaculate Conception	99
Litany of Our Lady of Sorrows	103
Litany of the Life of the Blessed Virgin Mary	106
Litany of the Sacred Heart of Mary	109

IV   Litanies in Honor of the Various Saints

Litany of St. Aloysius	115
Litany of St. Anne	118
Litany of Blessed Julia Billart	121
Litany of the Holy Angels	123
Litany of the Holy Angel Guardian	128
Litany of St. Stanislas Kotska	131
Litany of St. Vincent de Paul	134

Litany of Francis Xavier   138

V   Other Litanies

A Scriptural Litany   145
Litany of the Blessed Sacrament   149
Litany of the Children of Mary   153
Litany of the Faithful Departed   156
Litany for a Happy Death   162
Litany for Holy Communion   167
Litany of the Holy Cross   171
Litany of Penance   175
The Golden Litany   179

Bibliography   188

Introduction

How to Use Litanies in Prayer

Litanies are a wonderful expression of prayer; however, they can be somewhat intimidating to someone encountering them for the first time. To the unfamiliar, litanies can seem long, repetitive, and many associate them with a formal setting where they are often led by a priest. Can you actually use litanies in your personal devotions? Of course you can! Don't be intimidated.

First of all, many litanies are not as long as they seem at first. Yes, they contain many lines, but these lines are often short. Furthermore, different litanies themselves are different lengths - some are longer and others are shorter. However, most important of all is the subjective perception of length. Once you begin praying with litanies and get used to them, you will find that they are quite easy to fit with your regular personal prayers. Similar to those who feel like they don't have time to pray the rosary (but discover otherwise once they start), those who avoid litanies because of their length are often surprised how easy they are to work into your normal prayer schedule.

The issue of litanies seeming repetitive is again an issue of perception, as each line in a litany presents a unique aspect worthy of meditation. Naturally, there are repetitive elements, but also like the rosary, this repetition forms the basis for a rhythm of prayer and meditation on the litany's subject. Many litanies, in fact, express a highly developed theology that elaborates on divine attributes, truths of salvation, and the qualities of holiness.

The theology of litanies is expressed in diverse way depending on the litany and its subject. Litanies to God and the Persons of the Trinity teach us about the Divine characteristics, God's infinite Goodness, and His saving activity on our behalf. Litanies to the Blessed Virgin Mary are especially instructive about the nature and economy of grace, and Our Lady - as Queen of Heaven - is the exemplary example of our divine destiny. The litanies in honor of the various saints not only teach about the lives of the saints and their patronages, but also the different ways and titles of holiness that can be attained. These, therefore, are especially anagogic. Many liturgies also teach about salvation history and contain scriptural references that highlight the allegorical and anagogical levels of scripture. This brief explanation is, of course, not exhaustive. However, it is hopefully helpful as a starting point for contemplating more deeply the content of the various litanies.

Regarding the third issue, that many only experience litanies in formal settings, this is the easiest to resolve. Litanies are prayers like any other, and they can be prayed at any time. Just like other prayers, there are certain settings and situations that certain litanies are especially appropriate for, and there are six official litanies of the Church used in public worship. Five are reproduced here. The Litany of the Most Precious Blood of Jesus is omitted for copyright reasons; however, you can find this litany in the modern translation on the USCCB's website - an alternative for private devotion is supplied here.

Praying with litanies is easy. Litanies can be prayed at any time, but they are especially suited for use in novenas, in celebration of feast days, and for dedicating days of the week or seasons of the Church. Litanies are written to be prayed in the call-and-response format, but they can just as easily be prayed alone. Below, you will find an example of some suggested uses for litanies reproduced from *The Golden Manual*. Note, *The Golden Manual* was published in 1850, and so some adaptation may be made to fit the observances of the modern liturgical calendar. Feel free to adapt things as necessary in order to meet your needs for private devotion.

* * *

The subjoined Table shews the particular devotion by which it is a common practice to consecrate each day of the week :

- **Sunday …. To the Holy Trinity.**
- **Monday …. To the Holy Ghost.**
- **Tuesday …. To the Holy Angels.**
- **Wednesday …. To St. Joseph.**
- **Thursday …. To the Blessed Sacrament.**
- **Friday …. To the Passion of our Lord.**
- **Saturday …. To the Blessed Virgin.**

But, besides appropriating certain Litanies to the days of the week usually recommended for their use, it would be a profitable exercise, both for individuals and for families, to dedicate a week to Jesus and Mary, in the following way :

- **Sunday …. Litanies of the Holy Name of Jesus and of Loretto,**
- **Monday …. Litanies of the Incarnate Word and the Immaculate Conception.**
- **Tuesday …. Litanies of the Infant Jesus and of Loretto.**
- **Wednesday …. Litanies of the Holy Name of Jesus, and Holy Name of Mary.**

- **Thursday** .... *Litanies of the Life of Jesus, and Life of Mary.*
- **Friday** .... *Litanies of the Passion and of the Seven Dolours.*
- **Saturday** .... *Litanies of the Sacred Heart of Jesus, and Sacred Heart of Mary.*

Particular feasts will naturally suggest their corresponding devotions, — e.g. the several festivals of our Lord and his Blessed Mother, the Holy Angels, St. Joseph, etc. ; and no further guidance will be needed than that which is afforded by any Catholic Directory. But, for the readier fulfilment of the plan proposed, the following Table is prefixed, which gives the Litanies proper to each season in their order.

Table of Litanies Throughout Year.

- **Advent** .... *Litany of the Incarnate Word, and the Litany of Penance.*
- **Christmas** .... *Litany of the Infant Jesus*
- **Epiphany** .... *Litany of the Infant Jesus, and the Life of Jesus*
- **Septuagesima** .... *Litany of the Life of Jesus; and on Fridays, that of the Passion*
- **Lent** .... *Litany of Penance; and on Wednesdays and Fridays, that of the Passion*
- **Passion and Holy Weeks** .... *Litany of the Passion*
- **Maunday Thursday** .... *Litany of the Blessed Sacrament*
- **Good Friday** .... *Litany of the Passion and of the Holy Cross*
- **Easter** .... *Litany of the Resurrection*
- **Ascension Day to Whitsunday* [Pentecost]** .... *Litany of Jesus Glorified*
- **Whitsuntide* [Pentecost week]** .... *Litany of the Holy Ghost*
- **Trinity Sunday, and Sundays after Pentecost** .... *Litany of the Most Holy Trinity*
- **Corpus Christi** .... *Litany of the Blessed Sacrament*

[*Witsunday* and *Witsuntide* are terms designating Pentecost Sunday and the following week, respectively. These terms, of Saxon derivation, are sometimes used in England, Scotland, and Ireland.]

Devotion will contrive numerous combinations, by which the peculiar character of each day or season may be duly observed, and the several aspects of the Divine Mysteries receive their proper measure of attention and contemplation.

The Litany of the Saints ... may [also] very suitably be used on the festivals of those eminent Saints whose names are especially commemorated in [it].

Litanies, again, form appropriate devotions for particular Novenas, and for consecrating the several months of the year to some special object. To this end the following Table is given, shewing —

THE TIMES OF NOVENAS[1] AND OTHER DEVOTIONS,

which may be performed at discretion.

BEGINS.	ENDS.	NOVENAS, AND OTHER DEVOTIONS.
January	. . . .	Month of Devotion to the Holy Infancy.
Jan. 24 . .	Feb. 1 . .	Novena of the Purification of B. V. Mary.
Nine days before 2d Sunday of Epiphany .		,, ,, Holy Name of Jesus.
Feb. 1 . .	Feb. 9 . .	,, ,, Most Holy Trinity.
March		Month of Devotion to St. Joseph.
March 4 .	March 12 .	Novena of St. Francis Xavier.
,, 8 .	,, 16 .	,, St. Patrick.
,, 10 .	,, 18 .	,, St. Joseph.
,, 16 .	,, 24 .	,, the Annunciation of B. V. Mary
Thirteen Fridays before April 2		Devotion to St. Francis of Paula.
April 14 .	April 22 .	Novena of St. George.
May . .	. . . .	Month of Devotion to B. V. Mary.
Nine days before Whitsunday		Novena of the Holy Ghost.
June . .	. . . .	{ Month of Devotion to the Precious Blood of our Lord.
Nine days before the Feast of the S. Heart		Novena of the S. Heart of Jesus.
Six Sundays bef. June 21		Devotion to St. Aloysius Gonzaga.
June 20 . .	June 28 .	Novena of SS. Peter and Paul.
,, 21 . .	,, 30 .	,, St. Aloysius Gonzaga.
,, 17 . .	,, 25 .	,, St. Anne.
July 16 .	July 24 .	,, B. V. Mary of Mount Carmel.
August .	. . . .	Month of Devotion to the S. Heart of Mary.
Aug. 6 . .	Aug. 14 .	Novena of the Assumption of B. V. Mary.
,, 15 . .	,, 24 .	Ditto.
,, 30 . .	Sept. 7 .	Novena of the Nativity of B. V. Mary.
Sept. 20 .	,, 28 . .	,, St. Michael and Angel Guardians.
,, 26 .	Oct. 3 . .	,, St. Francis of Assisium.
October .	. . . .	Month of Devotion to the Holy Angels.
Oct. 7 . .	Oct. 15 . .	Novena of St. Teresa.
,, 24 . .	Nov. 1 . .	,, for the Souls in Purgatory.
November	. . . .	Month of Devotion for ditto.
Nov. 29 .	Dec. 7 . .	Novena of the Conception of B. V. Mary.
Dec. 16 .	,, 24 . .	,, ,, Nativity of our Lord.

[1] Many of these Novenas have Indulgences attached to them.

Table reproduced from The Golden Manual (1850), NB., *that certain feasts and/or their dates have changed in the new liturgical calendar. Additionally, the current indulgences of the Church and their requirements are specified in the* Manual of Indulgences: Norms and Grants. *Older indulgences, such as the practice of granting 100 days relief from purgatory for saying a certain prayer, may no longer be in force.*

I

Official Litanies of the Church

Litany of the Holy Name of Jesus

Lord have mercy upon us.
Lord have mercy upon us.
Christ have mercy upon us.
Christ have mercy upon us.
Lord have mercy upon us.
Lord have mercy upon us.
Christ hear us.
Christ graciously hear us.

[Respond: *Have mercy on us.*]
God the Father of heaven,
God the Son, Redeemer of the world,
God the Holy Ghost,
Holy Trinity, one God,
Jesus, Son of the living God,
Jesus, Splendor of the Father,
Jesus, Brightness of eternal Light,
Jesus, King of glory,
Jesus, the Sun of justice,
Jesus, Son of the Virgin Mary,
Jesus, most admirable,
Jesus, the mighty God,

Jesus, the Father of the world to come,
Jesus, the Angel of great counsel,
Jesus, most powerful,
Jesus, most patient,
Jesus, most obedient,
Jesus, meek and humble of heart
Jesus, Lover of Chastity,
Jesus, our Beloved,
Jesus, the God of peace,
Jesus, the Author of life,
Jesus, the Example of all virtues,
Jesus, the zealous Lover of souls,
Jesus, our God,
Jesus, our Refuge,
Jesus, the Father of the poor,
Jesus, the Treasurer of the faithful,
Jesus, the Good Shepherd,
Jesus, the true Light,
Jesus, the Eternal Wisdom,
Jesus, infinite Goodness,
Jesus, our Way and our Life,
Jesus, the Joy of Angels,
Jesus, the Joy of Angels,
Jesus, the Master of the Apostles,
Jesus, the Teacher of the Evangelists,
Jesus, the Strength of Martyrs,
Jesus, the Light of Confessors,
Jesus, the Purity of Virgins,
Jesus, the Crown of all Saints,

LITANY OF THE HOLY NAME OF JESUS

Be merciful,
> *Spare us, O Jesus.*
>
> Be merciful.
> *Graciously hear us, O Jesus.*

[Respond: *Lord Jesus, deliver us.*]
> From all sin,
> From thy wrath,
> From the snares of the devil,
> From the spirit of fornication,
> From everlasting death,
> From neglect of thy inspirations,
> Through the mystery of thy holy Incarnation,
> Through thy Nativity,
> Through thy Infancy,
> Through thy most divine Life,
> Through thy Labors,
> Through thine Agony and Passion,
> Through thy Cross and Dereliction,
> Through thy Weariness and Faintness,
> Through thy Death and Burial,
> Through thy Resurrection,
> Through thine Ascension,
> Through thy Joys,
> Through thy glory,

Lamb of God, who takes away the sins of the world.
> *Spare us, O Jesus,*
>
> Lamb of God, who takes away the sins of the world,
> *Graciously hear us, O Jesus.*
>
> Lamb of God, who takes away the sins of the world,

Have mercy on us, O Jesus.
Jesus, hear us.
Jesus, graciously hear us.

O Lord Jesus Christ, who hast said: "Ask, and ye shall receive; seek, and ye shall find; knock, and it shall be opened unto you" grant, we beseech thee, to us who ask the gift of thy divine love, that we may love thee with our whole heart, in word and work, and never cease from showing forth thy praise.

O God, who hast appointed thine only begotten Son the Savior of mankind, and hast commanded that he should be called Jesus; mercifully grant, that we may enjoy in heaven the blessed vision of Him, whose holy Name we venerate upon earth. Through the name our Lord.

Amen.

Litany of the Sacred Heart

Lord, have mercy
Lord, have mercy
Christ, have mercy
Christ, have mercy
Lord, have mercy
Lord, have mercy

[Respond: *Have mercy on us.*]
God our Father in heaven
God the Son, Redeemer of the world
God the Holy Spirit
Holy Trinity, one God
Heart of Jesus, Son of the eternal Father
Heart of Jesus, formed by the Holy Spirit in the womb of the Virgin Mother
Heart of Jesus, one with the eternal Word
Heart of Jesus, infinite in majesty
Heart of Jesus, holy temple of God
Heart of Jesus, tabernacle of the Most High
Heart of Jesus, house of God and gate of heaven
Heart of Jesus, aflame with love for us
Heart of Jesus, source of justice and love

Heart of Jesus, full of goodness and love
Heart of Jesus, well-spring of all virtue
Heart of Jesus, worthy of all praise
Heart of Jesus, king and center of all hearts
Heart of Jesus, treasure-house of wisdom and knowledge
Heart of Jesus, in whom there dwells the fullness of God
Heart of Jesus, in whom the Father is well pleased
Heart of Jesus, from whose fullness we have all received
Heart of Jesus, desire of the eternal hills
Heart of Jesus, patient and full of mercy
Heart of Jesus, generous to all who turn to you
Heart of Jesus, fountain of life and holiness
Heart of Jesus, atonement for our sins
Heart of Jesus, overwhelmed with insults
Heart of Jesus, broken for our sins
Heart of Jesus, obedient even to death
Heart of Jesus, pierced by a lance
Heart of Jesus, source of all consolation
Heart of Jesus, our life and resurrection
Heart of Jesus, our peace and reconciliation
Heart of Jesus, victim of our sins
Heart of Jesus, salvation of all who trust in you
Heart of Jesus, hope of all who die in you
Heart of Jesus, delight of all the saints

Lamb of God, you take away the sins of the world
have mercy on us
Lamb of God, you take away the sins of the world
have mercy on us
Lamb of God, you take away the sins of the world
have mercy on us

Jesus, gentle and humble of heart.
> *Touch our hearts and make them like your own.*

Let us pray.
> Grant, we pray, almighty God,
> that we, who glory in the Heart of your beloved Son
> and recall the wonders of his love for us,
> may be made worthy to receive
> an overflowing measure of grace
> from that fount of heavenly gifts.
> Through Christ our Lord.
> Amen.

Litany of the Blessed Virgin Mary (Litany of Loreto)

Lord, have mercy.
Lord, have mercy.
Christ have mercy.
Christ have mercy.
Lord have mercy.
Lord have mercy.

God the Father of heaven,
Have mercy on us.
God the Son, Redeemer of the world,
Have mercy on us.
God the Holy Spirit,
Have mercy on us.
Holy Trinity, one God,
Have mercy on us.

[Respond with: *Pray for us.*]
Holy Mary,
Holy Mother of God,
Holy Virgin of virgins,
Mother of Christ,

LITANY OF THE BLESSED VIRGIN MARY (LITANY OF LORETO)

Mother of the Church,
Mother of mercy,
Mother of divine grace,
Mother of hope,
Mother most pure,
Mother most chaste,
Mother inviolate,
Mother undefiled,
Mother most amiable,
Mother most admirable,
Mother of good counsel,
Mother of our Creator,
Mother of our Savior,
Virgin most prudent,
Virgin most venerable,
Virgin most renowned,
Virgin most powerful,
Virgin most merciful,
Virgin most faithful,
Mirror of justice,
Seat of wisdom,
Cause of our joy,
Spiritual vessel,
Vessel of honor,
Singular vessel of devotion,
Mystical rose,
Tower of David,
Tower of ivory,
House of gold,
Ark of the covenant,
Gate of heaven,

Morning star,
Health of the sick,
Refuge of sinners,
Comfort of Migrants,
Comforter of the afflicted,
Help of Christians,
Queen of Angels,
Queen of Patriarchs,
Queen of Prophets,
Queen of Apostles,
Queen of Martyrs,
Queen of Confessors,
Queen of Virgins,
Queen of all Saints,
Queen conceived without original sin,
Queen assumed into heaven,
Queen of the most holy Rosary,
Queen of Families,
Queen of Peace,

Lamb of God, you take away the sins of the world,
Spare us, O Lord.
Lamb of God, you take away the sins of the world,
Graciously hear us, O Lord.
Lamb of God, you take away the sins of the world,
Have mercy on us.

V. Pray for us, O holy Mother of God,
R. That we may be made worthy of the promises of Christ.

Let us pray,

Grant, we beseech you, Lord God, that we your servants may rejoice in continual health of mind and body and, by the glorious intercession of Blessed Mary, ever Virgin, may we be delivered from present sorrow to delight in joy eternal. Through Christ our Lord.

Amen.

Litany of the Saints

Lord have mercy.
Lord have mercy.
Christ have mercy.
Christ have mercy.
Lord have mercy.
Lord have mercy.
Christ hear us.
Christ graciously hear us

God, the Father of heaven,
Have mercy on us.
God the Son, Redeemer of the world,
Have mercy on us.
God, the Holy Spirit,
Have mercy on us.
Holy Trinity, One God,
Have mercy on us.

[Respond with: *Pray for us.*]
Holy Mary,
Holy Mother of God,
Holy Virgin of virgins,

Saint Michael,
Saint Gabriel,
Saint Raphael,
All ye holy angels and archangels,
All ye holy orders of blessed spirits,
Saint John the Baptist,
Saint Joseph,
All ye holy patriarchs and prophets.
Saint Peter,
Saint Paul,
Saint Andrew,
Saint James,
Saint John,
Saint Thomas,
Saint James,
Saint Philip,
Saint Bartholomew.
Saint Matthew,
Saint Simon,
Saint Thaddeus,
Saint Matthias,
Saint Barnabas,
Saint Luke,
Saint Mark,
All ye holy apostles and evangelists,
All ye holy disciples of our Lord.
All ye holy Innocents,
Saint Stephen,
Saint Lawrence,
Saint Vincent,
Saints Fabian and Sebastian,

Saints John and Paul,
Saints Cosmas and Damian,
Saints Gervase and Protase,
All ye holy martyrs,
Saint Sylvester,
Saint Gregory,
Saint Ambrose,
Saint Augustine.
Saint Jerome,
Saint Martin,
Saint Nicolas,
All ye holy bishops and confessors,
All ye holy doctors,
Saint Anthony,
Saint Benedict,
Saint Bernard,
Saint Dominic,
Saint Francis,
All ye holy priests and levites,
All ye holy monks and hermits.
Saint Mary Magdalen,
Saint Agatha,
Saint Lucy,
Saint Agnes,
Saint Cecily,
Saint Catherine,
Saint Anastasia,
All ye holy virgins and widows,

All ye holy men and women, Saints of God,
Make intercession for us.

Be merciful,
Spare us, O Lord.
Be merciful,
Graciously hear us, O Lord.

[Respond with: *O Lord, deliver us.*]
From all evil,
From all sin,
From Thy wrath,
From a sudden and unprovided death,
From the snares of the devil,
From anger, and hatred, and all ill will,
From the spirit of fornication,
From lightning and tempest,
From the scourge of earthquake.
From pestilence, famine and war,
From everlasting death,
Through the mystery of Thy holy Incarnation,
Through Thy coming,
Through Thy nativity,
Through Thy baptism and holy fasting,
Through Thy Cross and Passion,
Through Thy death and burial,
Through Thy holy Resurrection,
Through Thine admirable Ascension,
Through the coming of the Holy Spirit the Paraclete,
In the day of judgment,

[Respond with: *We beseech Thee, hear us.*]
We sinners,
That Thou wouldst spare us,

That Thou wouldst pardon us,
That Thou wouldst bring us to true penance,
That Thou wouldst govern and preserve Thy holy Church,
That Thou wouldst preserve our Apostolic Prelate, and all ecclesiastical orders in holy religion,
That Thou wouldst humble the enemies of Thy holy Church,
That Thou wouldst give peace and true concord to Christian kings and princes,
That Thou wouldst grant peace and unity to all Christian people,
That Thou wouldst bring back to the unity of the Church all those who have strayed away, and lead to the light of the Gospel all unbelievers,
That Thou wouldst confirm and preserve us in Thy holy service,
That Thou wouldst lift up our minds to heavenly desires,
That Thou wouldst render eternal blessings to all our benefactors,
That Thou wouldst deliver our souls, and the souls of our brethren, relations and benefactors, from eternal damnation,
That Thou wouldst give and preserve the fruit of the earth,
That Thou wouldst give eternal rest to all the faithful departed,
That Thou wouldst graciously hear us,
Son of God,

Lamb of God, Who takest away the sins of the world,
Spare us, O Lord.
Lamb of God, Who takest away the sins of the world,
Graciously hear us, O Lord.
Lamb of God, Who takest away the sins of the world,
Have mercy on us.

Christ hear us.
Christ, graciously hear us.

Lord, have mercy.
   Christ, have mercy.
   Lord, have mercy.

Our Father …

Psalm 69
   Deign, O Lord, to rescue me; O Lord, make haste to help me Let them be put to shame and confounded who seek my life. Let them be turned back in disgrace who desire my ruin. Let them retire in their shame who say to me, "Aha, aha!" But may all who seek Thee exult and be glad in Thee, And may those who love Thy salvation say ever, "God be glorified!" But I am afflicted and poor; O God, hasten to me! Thou art my help and my deliverer; O Lord, hold not back!
   Glory be to the Father, and to the Son, and to the Holy Ghost. As it was in the beginning, is now, and ever shall be, world without end.
   Save Thy servants.
   Amen.

Litany of St. Joseph

Lord have mercy.
Lord have mercy.
Christ have mercy.
Christ have mercy.
Lord have mercy.
Lord have mercy.
Christ hear us.
Christ graciously hear us.

God the Father of heaven,
Have mercy on us.
God the Son, Redeemer of the world,
Have mercy on us,
God the Holy Ghost,
Have mercy on us.
Holy Trinity, one God,
Have mercy on us.

[Respond with: *Pray for us.*]
Holy Mary, Spouse of Joseph,
Holy Joseph, Spouse of the Virgin Mary,
Nursing- father of Jesus,

Man according to God's own heart,
Faithful and prudent servant,
Guardian of the virginity of Mary,
Companion and solace of Mary,
Most pure in virginity.
Most profound in humility,
Most fervent in charity.
Most exalted in contemplation,
Who was declared to be a just man by the testimony of the Holy Ghost himself,
Who was enlightened above all the heavenly mysteries,
Who was the chosen minister of the counsels of the Most High,
Who was taught from above the mystery of the Incarnate Word,
Who did journey to Bethlehem with Mary thy Spouse, being great with child,
Who finding no place in the inn, did betake thyself to a stable,
Who was thought worthy to be present when Christ was born and laid in a manger,
Who did bear in thine arms the Son of God,
Who did receive the blood of Jesus at his Circumcision,
Who did present him to the Lord in the Temple, with Mary his Mother,
Who, at the warning of the Angel, did fly into Egypt with the Child and his Mother,
Who, when Herod was dead, did return with them into the land of Israel,
Who for three days, with Mary his Mother did seek sorrowing the Child Jesus, when he was last at Jerusalem,
Who, after three days, did find him with joy sitting in the midst of the Doctors,
Who had the Lord of lords subject to thee on the earth,

Who was the happy witness of his hidden life and sacred words,
Who did die in the arms of Jesus and Mary,
Whose praise is in the Gospel: The Husband of Mary, of whom was born Jesus,
Humble imitator of the Incarnate Word,
Powerful support of the Church,

Our advocate,
St. Joseph, hear us.
Our patron,
St. Joseph, graciously hear us.

[Respond with: *St. Joseph, hear us.*]
In all our necessities, In all our distresses,
In the our of death,
Through thy most chaste espousals,
Through thy paternal care and fidelity,
Through thy love of Jesus and Mary,
Through thy labors and toils,
Through all thy virtues,
Through thy exalted honor and eternal blessedness,
Through thy faithful intercession,

We, thy clients,
Beseech thee, hear us.

[Respond with: *We beseech thee, hear us.*]
That thou wouldst vouchsafe to obtain for us, from Jesus, the pardon of our sins,
That thou wouldst vouchsafe to commend us faithfully to Jesus and Mary,

That thou wouldst vouchsafe to obtain for all, both Virgins and married, the chastity belonging to their state,

That thou wouldst vouchsafe to obtain for all congregations perfect love and concord,

That thou wouldst vouchsafe to direct all rulers and prelates in the government of their subjects,

That thou wouldst vouchsafe to assist all parents in the Christian education of their children,

That thou wouldst vouchsafe to protect all those that rely upon thy patronage,

That thou wouldst vouchsafe to support, with thy paternal help, all congregations instituted under thy name and patronage,

That thou wouldst vouchsafe to visit and stand by us, with Jesus and Mary, in the last moment of our life,

That thou wouldst vouchsafe to succor, by thy prayers and intercession, all the faithful departed,

O chaste Spouse of Mary.

O faithful Nursing-father of Jesus,

Holy Joseph,

Lamb of God who takes away the sins of the world,
Spare us, O Lord.
Lamb of God, who takes away the sins of the world,
Graciously hear us, O Lord.
Lamb of God, who takes away the sins of the world,
Have mercy on us.

Christ hear us,
Christ graciously hear us.

V. Pray for us, O blessed Joseph.

R. That we may be made worthy of the promises of Christ.

Let us Pray:

O God, who didst choose St. Joseph to be the Spouse of blessed Mary ever Virgin, and to be the Guardian and Nursing father of thy beloved Son, our Lord Jesus Christ; we humbly beseech thee to grant us, through his patronage and merits, such purity of mind and body, that, being clean from every stain, and clothed with the true marriage-garment, we may, by thy great mercy, be admitted to the heavenly nuptials. Through the same Christ our Lord.

Amen.

II

Litanies to the Persons of the Holy Trinity

Litany of the Most Holy Trinity

Lord, have mercy.
  Lord, have mercy.
  Christ, have mercy.
  Christ, have mercy.
  Lord, have mercy.
  Lord, have mercy.

Blessed Trinity,
  Hear us.

[Respond with: *Have mercy on us.*]
  God, the Father of heaven,
  God, the Son, Redeemer of the world,
  God, the Holy Ghost,
  Holy Trinity, one God,
  Father, from Whom are all things,
  Son, through Whom are all things,
  Holy Ghost, in Whom are all things,
  Holy and undivided Trinity,
  Father everlasting,
  Only-begotten Son of the Father,
  Spirit, Who proceedest from the Father and the Son,

Co-eternal Majesty of three divine Persons,
Father, the Creator,
Son, the Redeemer,
Holy Ghost, the Comforter,
Holy, holy, holy, Lord God of hosts,
Who art. Who wast, and Who art to come,
God, most High, Who inhabitest eternity,
To Whom alone are due all honor and glory,
Power infinite,
Wisdom incomprehensible,
Love unspeakable,

Be merciful.
Spare us, O holy Trinity.
Be merciful.
Graciously hear us, O holy Trinity.

[Respond with: *Deliver us, O Holy Trinity.*]
   From all evil,
   From all sin,
   From all pride,
   From all love of riches,
   From all uncleanness,
   From all sloth,
   From all inordinate affection,
   From all envy and malice,
   From all anger and impatience,
   From every thought, word, and deed, contrary to Thy holy law,
   From Thy everlasting malediction,
   Through Thy almighty power,
   Through Thy loving kindness,

LITANY OF THE MOST HOLY TRINITY

Through the inexhaustible treasures of Thy goodness and love,
Through the depths of Thy wisdom and knowledge.
Through all Thy unspeakable perfections,

We sinners,
Beseech Thee, hear us.

[Respond with: *We beseech Thee, hear us.*]
That we may ever serve Thee alone,
That we may worship Thee in spirit and in truth,
That we may love Thee with all our heart, with all our soul, and with all our strength.
That, for Thy sake we may love our neighbor as ourselves,
That we may faithfully keep Thy holy commandments,
That we may never defile our bodies and our souls with sin,
That we may go from grace to grace, and from virtue to virtue,
That we may finally enjoy the sight of Thee in glory,
That Thou wouldst vouchsafe to hear us,

O blessed Trinity,
We beseech Thee, deliver us.
O blessed Trinity,
We beseech Thee, save us.
O blessed Trinity,
Have mercy on us.

Lord, have mercy.
Christ, have mercy.
Lord, have mercy.

V. Blessed art Thou, O Lord, in the firmament of heaven.
R. And worthy to be praised and magnified forever.

Let us pray

Almighty and everlasting God, Who hast given to Thy servants, in the confession of the true faith, to bear witness to the glory of the eternal Trinity, and in the power of its majesty to adore the unity; grant, we beseech Thee, that, by steadfastness in this faith, we may ever be defended from all adversities: Through Our Lord Jesus Christ. Amen.

Litany of the Incarnate Word

Lord have mercy.
Lord have mercy.
Christ have mercy.
Christ have mercy.
Lord have mercy.
Lord have mercy.

[Respond with: *Have mercy on us.*]
God the Father of heaven,
God the Son, Redeemer of the world,
God the Holy Ghost,
Holy Trinity, one God,
Word made flesh,
Word full of grace and truth,
God by whom all things were made,
Lord God of Israel, blessed for evermore.
Only-begotten Son of God,
Saviour, Christ, and Lord,
Great God, Son of the Most High,
God with us, Emmanuel,
Only-begotten Son, who art in the bosom of the ✠ Father,
Well-beloved Son of God, in whom the Father is well pleased,

Wisdom set up from all eternity,
Image of the invisible God,
Whose Name is above every name,
Who upholdest all things by the word of thy power, Beginning of the creation of God,
First-born of every creature, First-born among many brethren,
Heir of all things,
Flower of the field, and Lily of the valleys,
Bud of justice,
Angel of the Lord,
Angel of the Testament,
Star arisen out of Jacob,
Lion of the tribe of Judah, Rod of Jesse,
Son of David,
Son of man,
Jesus of Nazareth,
Meek and humble of heart,
Good Shepherd, who givest thy life for thy sheep,
Shepherd and Bishop of our souls,
Saint of saints,
Prince of pastors,
Great Prophet, mighty in word and work,
Who wast sent to preach the gospel to the poor,
The Lord our lawgiver,
Light of the world,
True Light, which enlightenest every man that cometh into the world,
Key of David,
Ark of the testament.
Living Stone, elect of God, Stone that art become the head of the corner,
Stone of foundation laid in the midst of Sion,

Prince of the kings of the earth,
Master and Lord,
King of kings and Lord of lords,
Man of sorrows, acquainted with infirmity,
Who hast truly borne our infirmities,
By whose bruises we are healed,
Lamb without blemish,
Lamb slain from the beginning of the world.
Our Prince and Saviour,
My Lord and my God, Salvation of God sent to the Gentiles,
The Propitiation for our sins,
The Apostle and High Priest of our confession,
The one Mediator between God and man,
Mediator of the New Testament,
Author and Finisher of faith,
First-begotten of the dead. The Resurrection and the Life,
The Pasch and nourishment of our souls,
Who hast the keys of death and hell,
Our Advocate with the Father,
The Temple and the Lamp of the holy city,
Hope of mortals,
Tree of life,
Light of life,
Fountain of life,
The Beginning and the End,
Judge of the living and the dead,
God blessed for ever,

Lamb of God, who takest away the sins of the world,
   Spare us, O Lord.
   Lamb of God, who takest away the sins of the world,

Graciously hear us, O Lord.
Lamb of God, who takest away the sins of the world,
Grant us thy peace.

Christ hear us.
Christ graciously hear us.

Let us pray.

O God, who, by thy co-eternal Wisdom, didst make man when he was not, and mercifully restore him when he was lost; grant, we beseech thee, that by the inspiration of the same Wisdom, we may both love thee with our whole soul, and fly to thee with our whole heart. Through the same Jesus Christ our Lord. Amen.

Litany of the Infant Jesus

Lord have mercy.
Lord have mercy.
Christ have mercy.
Christ have mercy.
Lord have mercy.
Lord have mercy.

Infant Jesus,
Hear us.
Infant Jesus ,
Graciously hear us.

[Respond with: *Have mercy on us.*]
God the Father of heaven,
God the Son, Redeemer of the world,
God the Holy Ghost,
Holy Trinity, one God,
Infant Jesus,
Infant, very God,
Infant, Son of the living God,
Infant, Son of the Virgin Mary,
Infant, begotten before the morning star,

Infant, Word made flesh, Infant, Wisdom of thy Father,
Infant, Purity of thy Mother,
Infant, only Son of thy Father,
Infant, First-Born of thyMother,
Infant, Image of thy Father, Infant, Creator of thy Mother,
Infant, Splendour of thy Father,
Infant, Honour of thy Mother,
Infant, equal to thy Father,
Infant, subject to thy Mother,
Infant, Joy of thy Father,
Infant, Riches of thy Mother,
Infant, Gift of thy Father,
Infant, Offering of thy Mother,
Infant, precious Fruit of a Virgin,
Infant, Creator of man,
Infant, Power of God,
Infant, our God,
Infant, our Brother,
Infant, perfect Man from thy Conception,
Infant, ancient in wisdom from thy Childhood,
Infant, Father of ages.
Infant of days,
Infant, giving life, and nourished at the breast,
Infant, Eternal Word, and making thyself dumb,
Infant, weeping in the crib,
Infant, thundering in the heavens,
Infant, Terror of hell,
Infant, Joy of paradise,
Infant, dreaded by tyrants,
Infant, desired by the Magi,
Infant, exiled from thy people,

LITANY OF THE INFANT JESUS

Infant, King in exile,
Infant, Destroyer of idols,
Infant, Vindicator of the glory of God,
Infant, strong in weakness,
Infant, powerful in abasement,
Infant, Treasure of grace,
Infant, Fountain of love,
Infant, Author of the blessings of heaven,
Infant, Repairer of the evils of earth,
Infant, Head of the Angels,
Infant, Stem of the Patriarchs,
Infant, Word of the Prophets,
Infant, Expectation of nations,
Infant, Joy of the shepherds,
Infant, Light of the Magi,
Infant, Salvation of children.
Infant, Hope of the just,
Infant, Teacher of Doctors,
Infant, Firstfruits of the Saints,

Be merciful.
Spare us, O Infant Jesus.
Be merciful.
Graciously hear us , O Infant Jesus.

[Respond with: *Infant Jesus, deliver us.*]
From the bondage of the children of Adam,
From the slavery of the devil,
From the corruption of the world,
From the lust of the flesh,
From the pride of life,

From an immoderate desire of knowledge,
From blindness of mind,
From perversity of will,
From our sins,
Through thy most pure Conception,
Through thy most humble Birth,
Through thy Tears,
Through thy most painful Circumcision,
Through thy most glorious Epiphany,
Through thy most devout a Presentation,
Through thy most innocent Conversation in the world,
Through thy most holy Life,
Through thy Poverty,
Through thy Sorrows,
Through thy Labours and Travails,

Lamb of God, who takest away the sins of the world.
Spare us, O Infant Jesus.
Lamb of God, who takest away the sins of the world,
Graciously hear us, O Infant Jesus.
Lamb of God, who takest away the sins of the world,
Have mercy on us, O Infant Jesus.

Infant Jesus,
Hear us.
Infant Jesus,
Graciously hear us.

Let us pray.
O Lord Jesus, who didst vouchsafe so to annihilate the greatness of thy Incarnate Divinity and most Sacred Humanity, as to be born

in time, and become a little child; grant that we may acknowledge Infinite Wisdom in the silence of a child, Power in weakness, Majesty in abasement; so that, adoring thy humiliations on earth, we may contemplate thy glories in heaven. Who, with the Father and the Holy Ghost, livest and reignest, God, for ever and ever. Amen.

Litany of the Life of Jesus Christ

Lord have mercy.
Lord have mercy.
Christ have mercy.
Christ have mercy.
Christ hear us.
Christ graciously hear us.

[Respond with: *Have mercy on us.*]
God the Father of heaven,
God the Son, Redeemer of the world,
God the Holy Ghost,
Holy Trinity, one God,
Jesus, sent into the world by the Father,
Jesus, conceived by the Holy Ghost,
Jesus, who didst put on the form of a servant,
Jesus, born of the Virgin Mary,
Jesus, adored by thy Mother,
Jesus, wrapped in swaddling clothes,
Jesus, cradled in a manger,
Jesus, nourished at a virgin's breast,
Jesus, manifesting thyself to shepherds,
Jesus, submitting to the law of circumcision,

LITANY OF THE LIFE OF JESUS CHRIST

Jesus, adored by the Magi,
Jesus, presented in the Temple,
Jesus, received into the arras of the just Simeon,
Jesus, exiled into Egypt,
Jesus, persecuted by Herod,
Jesus, brought up at Nazareth,
Jesus, found in the Temple in the midst of the Doctors,
Jesus, subject to thy Parents,
Jesus, baptised by John,
Jesus, tempted in the desert,
Jesus, choosing for thy disciples the poor and ignorant,
Jesus, assisting the afflicted,
Jesus, transfigured on the mountain,
Jesus, weeping over Jerusalem,
Jesus, entering Jerusalem as King of Peace,
Jesus, driving the buyers and sellers from the Temple,
Jesus, washing thy disciples feet,
Jesus, eating the Pasch with thy disciples,
Jesus, giving thy Body for food, and thy Blood for drink,
Jesus, praying in the Garden of Olives,
Jesus betrayed by Judas,
Jesus, hated and spitefully treated,
Jesus, scourged and crowned with thorns,
Jesus, going up to Calvary,
Jesus, crucified between two thieves,
Jesus, made the scorn of men,
Jesus, dying upon the cross, Jesus, after thy death, going down into hell.
Jesus, rising again for our justification,
Jesus, ascending into heaven,
Jesus, sitting down at the right hand of the Father,

Jesus, crowned with glory and honour,
Jesus, sending down on thy disciples the Holy Ghost the Paraclete,
Jesus, preparing for the just an eternal kingdom,

Lamb of God, who takest away the sins of the world,
Spare us , O Lord Jesus.
Lamb of God, who takest away the sins of the world,
Graciously hear us, O Lord Jesus.
Lamb of God, who takest away the sins of the world,
Have mercy on us, O Lord Jesus.

Christ hear us.
Christ graciously hear us.

Let us pray.

O God, who wiliest not the death, but the conversion of sinners; look favourably on thy people, who, honouring the humiliations and the glories of thy holy life, fly to thy refuge with a contrite heart; and in thy merciful kindness turn from us war, famine, pestilence, and all the other scourges of thine anger. Who livest and reignest for ever and ever. Amen.

Litany of the Passion

Lord have mercy on us.
Lord have mercy on us.
Christ, have mercy on us.
Christ, have mercy on us.
Lord, have mercy on us.
Lord, have mercy on us.

Christ, hear us.
Christ, graciously hear us.

[Respond with: *Have mercy on us.*]
   God, the Father of heaven,
   God, the Son, Redeemer of the world,
   God, the Holy Ghost,
   Holy Trinity, one God,
   Jesus, the eternal Wisdom,
   Jesus, sold for thirty pieces of silver,
   Jesus, prostrate on the ground in prayer,
   Jesus, strengthened by an angel,
   Jesus, in Thine agony bathed in a bloody sweat,
   Jesus, betrayed by Judas with a kiss,
   Jesus, bound by the soldiers,

Jesus, forsaken by Thy disciples,
Jesus, brought before Annas and Caiphas,
Jesus, struck in the face by a servant,
Jesus, accused by false witnesses,
Jesus, declared guilty of death,
Jesus, spat upon,
Jesus, blindfolded,
Jesus, smitten on the cheek,
Jesus, thrice denied by Peter,
Jesus, delivered up to Pilate,
Jesus, despised and mocked by Herod,
Jesus, clothed in a white garment,
Jesus, rejected for Barabbas,
Jesus, torn with scourges,
Jesus, bruised for our sins,
Jesus, esteemed a leper,
Jesus, covered with a purple robe,
Jesus, crowned with thorns,
Jesus, struck with a reed upon the head,
Jesus, demanded for crucifixion by the Jews,
Jesus, condemned to an ignominious death,
Jesus, given up to the will of Thine enemies,
Jesus, loaded with the heavy weight of the cross,
Jesus, led like a sheep to slaughter,
Jesus, stripped of Thy garments,
Jesus, fastened with nails to the cross,
Jesus, reviled by the malefactors,
Jesus, promising paradise to the penitent thief,
Jesus, commending St. John to Thy mother as her son,
Jesus, declaring Thyself forsaken by Thy Father,
Jesus, in Thy thirst given gall and vinegar to drink,

LITANY OF THE PASSION

Jesus, testifying that all things written concerning Thee were accomplished,
Jesus, commending Thy spirit into the hands of Thy Father,
Jesus, obedient even to the death of the cross,
Jesus, pierced with a lance,
Jesus, made a propitiation for us,
Jesus, taken down from the cross,
Jesus, laid in the sepulcher,
Jesus, rising gloriously from the dead,
Jesus, ascending into heaven,
Jesus, our advocate with the Father,
Jesus, sending down on Thy disciples the Holy Ghost, the Paraclete,
Jesus, exalting Thy mother above the choirs of angels,
Jesus, Who shalt come to judge the living and the dead,

Be merciful,
Spare us, O Lord.
Be merciful,
Graciously hear us, O Lord.

[Respond with: *Lord Jesus, deliver us.*]
From all evil,
From all sin,
From anger, hatred, and every evil will,
From war, famine, and pestilence,
From all dangers of mind and body,
From everlasting death,
Through Thy most pure conception,
Through Thy miraculous nativity,
Through Thy humble circumcision,
Through Thy baptism and holy fasting,

Through Thy labors and watchings,
Through Thy cruel scourging and crowning,
Through Thy thirst, and tears, and nakedness,
Through Thy precious death and cross,
Through Thy glorious resurrection and ascension.
Through Thy sending forth the Paraclete, the Holy Ghost,
In the day of judgment,

[Respond with: *We beseech Thee, hear us.*]

We sinners beseech Thee, hear us.

That Thou wouldst spare us,

That Thou wouldst pardon us,

That Thou wouldst vouchsafe to bring us to true penance,

That Thou wouldst vouchsafe mercifully to pour into our hearts the grace of the Holy Spirit,

That Thou wouldst vouchsafe to defend and propagate Thy holy Church,

That Thou wouldst vouchsafe to preserve and prosper all Eucharistic associations.

That Thou wouldst vouchsafe to bestow upon us true peace,

That Thou wouldst vouchsafe to give us perseverance in grace and in Thy holy service,

That Thou wouldst vouchsafe to kindle in our hearts that divine fire which consumes the saints and transforms them into Thee,

That Thou wouldst vouchsafe to unite us to the company of Thy saints,

That Thou wouldst vouchsafe graciously to hear us,

Lamb of God, Who takest away the sins of the world,
Spare us, O Lord.

Lamb of God, Who takest away the sins of the world,

Graciously hear us, O Lord.
Lamb of God, Who takest away the sins of the world,
Have mercy on us, O Lord.

Christ, hear us;
Christ, graciously hear us.

V. We adore Thee, O Christ, and praise Thee:
R. Because by Thy holy cross Thou hast redeemed the world.

Let us pray

O God, Who to redeem the world didst vouchsafe to be born amongst men, to be circumcised, rejected by the Jews, betrayed by the traitor Judas with a kiss, to be bound with cords, and as an innocent lamb to be led to the slaughter; who didst suffer Thyself to be shamelessly exposed to the gaze of Annas, Caiphas, Pilate, and Herod; to be accused by false witnesses, tormented by scourges and insults, crowned with thorns, smitten with blows, defiled with spittings, to have Thy divine countenance covered, to be struck with a reed, to be stripped of Thy clothes, nailed to and raised high upon a cross between two thieves, to be given gall and vinegar to drink, and then pierced with a lance; do Thou, O Lord, by these most sacred sufferings, which I, unworthy as I am, yet dare to contemplate, by Thy holy cross, and by Thy bitter death, free me from the pains of hell, and vouchsafe to bring me to paradise, whither Thou didst lead the thief who was crucified with Thee, my Jesus, who with the Father and the Holy Ghost livest and reignest God forever and ever. Amen.

Litany of the Resurrection

Lord have mercy.
Lord have mercy.
Christ have mercy.
Christ have mercy.
Lord have mercy.
Lord have mercy.

Christ hear us.
Christ graciously hear us.

[Respond with: *Have mercy on us.*]
God the Father of heaven,
God the Son, Redeemer of the world,
God the Holy Ghost,
Holy Trinity, one God,
Jesus, Redeemer of mankind,
Jesus, who hast cleansed us by thy blood,
Jesus, Conqueror of sin and death,
Jesus, the Holy One and the Just,
Jesus, the First-Born from the dead,
Jesus, the Second Adam,
Jesus, the Resurrection and the Life,

LITANY OF THE RESURRECTION

Jesus, the Author of life,
Jesus, the Author of our salvation,
Jesus, the God of Abraham, and of Isaac, and of Jacob,
Jesus, who by death didst destroy him who had the empire of death,
Jesus, who didst bring life and immortality to light,
Jesus, who didst lay down thy life for thy sheep,
Jesus, who hadst power to lay it down, and hadst power to take it up again,
Jesus, who, after three days, didst rise again from the dead,
Jesus, who didst rise very early in the morning on the first day of the week,
Jesus, who didst hasten to visit thy blessed Mother in her solitude,
Jesus, who didst appear to Mary Magdalen while it was yet dark,
Jesus, who didst graciously console her in her affliction,
Jesus, who didst send thy angels to announce to the women, that thou wast risen as thou hadst said,
Jesus, who didst suffer thyself to be seen of the women, and to be adored by them,
Jesus, who didst appear to Peter, the chief of the apostles,
Jesus, who didst appear, in another shape, to the two disciples going to Emmaus,
Jesus, who didst make thyself known unto them in the breaking of bread,
Jesus, who didst appear to the eleven, saying, Peace be unto you,
Jesus, who didst breathe upon them, and give unto them the Holy Ghost,
Jesus, who didst confirm the faith of Thomas, by shewing unto him thy hands and thy feet,
Jesus, who didst shew thyself again to thy disciples, at the sea of Tiberias,
Jesus, who didst commission Peter to feed thy lambs and thy sheep,

Jesus, who didst converse with thy disciples, upon the mountain of Galilee, Jesus, who wast seen by more than five hundred brethren at once,

Jesus, who wast seen by James,

Jesus, who didst go in and out among thy apostles, speaking to them of the kingdom of God, and eating with them,

Jesus, who didst lead them out as far as Bethany, and, while they looked on, wast carried up to heaven,

Jesus, who shalt come again with great power and glory, to judge the living and the dead,

Jesus, Son of God,

We sinners,
Beseech thee, hear us.

[Respond with: *We beseech Thee, hear us.*]

That we may put off the old man with his acts,

That we may put on the new man, who is created in justice and holiness of truth,

That we may walk in newness of life,

That we may grow in grace, and in the knowledge of thee,

That we may persevere unto the end,

That, having risen with thee, we may die no more,

That we may attain unto the resurrection of the just,

That thou wouldst vouchsafe to feed us continually with the bread of life,

That thou wouldst reform the body of our lowliness, and make it like unto the body of thy glory.

That we may have confidence before thee at thy coming

That we may behold thy face with joy,

That we may be placed on thy right hand in the judgment,

That we may hear those words of joy : Come, ye blessed of my Father, possess ye the kingdom prepared for you from the foundation of the world,
   That thou wouldst give us part in thy heavenly glory,
   That thou wouldst give rest and peace to the faithful departed,
   That with them we may obtain everlasting life,
   That we may be with thee always, for ever and ever,

Lamb of God, who takest away the sins of the world.
Spare us, O Lord,
Lamb of God, who takest away the sins of the world,
Graciously hear us, O Lord.
Lamb of God, who takest away the sins of the world,
Have mercy on us.

Christ hear us.
Christ graciously hear us.

V. Christ is risen. Alleluia.
   R. He is risen indeed, and hath appeared unto Simon. Alleluia.

Let us pray.
   O God, who, by thine only- begotten Son, hast (this day) opened the passage to eternity, through his victory over death ; vouchsafe, we beseech thee, so to confirm us by thy grace, that we may walk in all our ways like those who have been re- deemed from sin. Through the same Jesus Christ our Lord. Amen

Litany of Jesus Glorified

Lord have mercy.
> *Lord have mercy.*
> Christ have mercy.
> *Christ have mercy.*
> Lord have mercy.
> *Lord have mercy.*

Christ hear us.
> *Christ graciously hear us.*

[Respond with: *Have mercy on us.*]
> God the Father of heaven,
> God the Son, Redeemer of the world,
> God the Holy Ghost,
> Holy Trinity, one God,
> Jesus, King of Glory ,
> Jesus, Lord and Christ,
> Jesus, Prince and Saviour,
> Jesus, blessed and only mighty,
> Jesus, who only hast immortality,
> Jesus, who didst ascend into heaven,
> Jesus, who didst ascend above the stars into the heaven of heavens,

LITANY OF JESUS GLORIFIED

Jesus, who didst ascend to thy Father and our Father, to thy God and our God,

Jesus, who ledst captivity captive,

Jesus, who despoiledst principalities and powers, triumphing over them,

Jesus, who art exalted by the right hand of God,

Jesus, who art exalted far above all principality and power,

Jesus, to whom all power is given in heaven and earth,

Jesus, who art seated at the right hand of the Father,

Jesus, who art crowned with glory and honour,

Jesus, who art glorified with the glory which thou hadst with the Father before the world was,

Jesus, who art glorified, in thy Sacred Humanity, at the right hand of the Majesty on high,

Jesus, who must reign till thou hast put all things under thy feet,

Jesus, whose throne is for ever and ever,

Jesus, who art adored by all the Angels of God,

Jesus, who art anointed with the oil of gladness above thy fellows,

Jesus, who art the happiness of the Blessed, Jesus, in whose presence is life,

Jesus, who hast opened the kingdom of heaven to all believers,

Jesus, who hast entered into heaven itself for us, Jesus, the Mediator of the New Testament,

Jesus, our High Priest for ever, according to the order of Melchisedech,

Jesus, who always livest to make intercession for us, Jesus, who art able to save for ever those that come unto God by thee,

Jesus, Head over all the Church,

Jesus, who didst send down the Holy Ghost on thy disciples.

Jesus, who didst promise that whatsoever we asked in thy name thou wouldst do it,

Jesus, who art gone up into heaven, and art present with us in the Sacrament of the Altar,

Jesus, who didst assume thy blessed Mother with glory into heaven,

Jesus, who didst crown her with the brightest diadem of glory,

Jesus, who art gone to prepare a place for us,

Jesus, who shalt come again in like manner as them wentest away,

Jesus, who didst promise new heavens and a new earth, wherein dwelleth justice,

Jesus, who livest for ever, Jesus, Son of God,

We sinners,
Beseech thee, hear us.

[Respond with: *We beseech Thee, hear us.*]

That we may seek the things that are above, and not the things that are upon earth.

That thou wouldst cleanse our consciences from dead works to serve the living God,

That we may live the rest of our time in the flesh, not after the desires of men, but according to the will of God,

That thou wouldst dwell in our hearts by faith,

That thou wouldst come unto us, and make thy abode with us,

That we may hold fast the confession of our hope without wavering.

That thou wouldst pour down thy benedictions upon thy Church,

That thou wouldst order all things for the good of them that love thee,

That thou wouldst draw all men unto thee,

That thou wouldst fill our hearts with love and devotion to thy most holy Mother,

That thou wouldst give us confidence in the prayers of all thy Saints,

That thou wouldst come again and take us to thyself, that where thou

LITANY OF JESUS GLORIFIED

art, we may be also,
> That, when thou shalt appear, we may receive a never-fading crown of glory.
> That we may behold thy glory,
> That in thy light we may see light,
> That thou wouldst have mercy on the souls of the faithful departed.
> That thou wouldst let the light of thy countenance shine upon them.
> That thou wouldst admit them to the joy of the beatific vision,
> That thou wouldst hasten the day of thy appearing,
> That thou wouldst hear us from thy holy place,

Lamb of God, who takest away the sins of the world,
> *Spare us, O Lord.*

Lamb of God, who takest away the sins of the world,
> *Graciously hear us, O Lord.*

Lamb of God, who takest away the sins of the world,
> *Have mercy on us.*

Christ hear us.
> *Christ graciously hear us.*

V. God is ascended with jubilee. Alleluia.
> **R.** And the Lord with the sound of the trumpet. Alleluia.

Let us pray.
> Grant, we beseech thee, Almighty God, that we who believe that thine only begotten Son hath ascended [On Easter add: ***this day***] into heaven, may ourselves also in heart and mind thither ascend, and dwell in heavenly places. Through the same Lord, etc. Amen.

Litany of the Precious Blood of the Sacred Heart of Jesus

Lord, have mercy on us.
  Christ, have mercy on us.
  Lord, have mercy on us.

Jesus, hear us
Jesus, graciously hear us.

[Respond with: *Have mercy on us.*]
  God the Father of heaven.
  God the Son, Redeemer of the world,
  God the Holy Ghost,
  Holy Trinity, one God,
  Jesus, who for love of us wast crucified, and didst shed all thy blood,

O precious blood, springing from the sacred heart of Jesus, *Flow upon us.*
  Precious blood, vast sea of divine mercy, *Overwhelm us.*
  Precious blood, most pure offering, *Reconcile us.*
  Precious blood, pledge of immortality, *Give us joy.*
  Precious blood, sweet refreshment of holy souls, *Comfort us.*
  Precious blood, inexhaustible treasure, *Enrich us.*

LITANY OF THE PRECIOUS BLOOD OF THE SACRED HEART OF JESUS

Precious blood, furnace of love, *Inflame us.*
Precious blood, sweet delight of the faithful, *Charm us.*
Precious blood, fount of chastity, *Purify us.*
Precious blood, shed by the stroke of the lance which opened to us the heart of Jesus, *Enlighten us.*
Precious blood, the hope and refuge of sinners, *Answer for us.*
Precious blood, the seed of Christians, *Multiply us.*
Precious blood, admiration of the angels, *Exalt us.*
Precious blood, the love and the joy of the seraphim. *Inflame us.*
Precious blood, faith of the patriarchs, *Enlighten us.*
Precious blood, hope of the prophets, *Confirm us.*
Precious blood charity of the apostles, *Inflame us.*
Precious blood, strength of martyrs, *Sustain us.*
Precious blood, reward of confessors, *Animate us.*
Precious blood, beauty of virgins, *Adorn us.*
Precious blood, delight of all the saints, *Strengthen us.*

Lamb of God, who takest away the sins of the world,
Spare us, O Lord.
Lamb of God, who takest away the sins of the world,
Hear us, O Lord.
Lamb of God, who takest away the sins of the world,
Have mercy upon us.

Anthem.
The fountains of the vast abyss are poured forth abundantly from the heart of Jesus, and the gates thereof are opened to us.

V. Hasten, O thirsty soul,
  R. And wash thyself seven times in this Jordan of blood.

Let us pray.

  O Lord Jesus Christ, who hast vouchsafed to shed thy precious blood freely for us, make us speedily feel its admirable virtue, and salutary help, by its constant application to our souls, who livest and reignest, world without end. Amen

Litanies of the Sacred Heart of Jesus for Every Day of the Week

MONDAY: Litany of the Sacred Heart of the Child Jesus

Lord, have mercy on us.
    Christ, have mercy on us.
    Lord, have mercy on us.

Christ, hear us,
    Christ, graciously hear us.

[Respond with: *Have mercy on us.*]
    God the Father of heaven,
    God the Son, Redeemer of the world,
    God the Holy Ghost,
    Holy Trinity, one God,
    Heart of the Child Jesus,
    Heart of Jesus, formed in the womb of the blessed Virgin Mary,
    Heart of Jesus, reposing on the bosom of Mary,

Heart of Jesus, nourished with the milk of Mary,
Heart of Jesus, in whom thy Father was alone pleased,
Heart of Jesus, hypostatically united to the Son of God,
Heart of Jesus, wonderful work of the Holy Ghost,
Heart of Jesus, tabernacle of the blessed Trinity,
Heart of Jesus, furnace of love,
Heart of Jesus, throne of love,
Heart of Jesus, dwelling of love and justice. Heart of Jesus, source of sweetness,
Heart of Jesus, powerful in weakness.
Heart of Jesus, miracle of obedience.
Heart of Jesus, abyss of humility,
Heart of Jesus, ocean of goodness.
Heart of Jesus, sweet centre of my heart, Heart of Jesus, my sovereign felicity,
Heart of Jesus, which love has disarmed. Heart of Jesus, treasure opened to us,
Heart of Jesus, source of benedictions,
Heart of Jesus, principle of sanctity,
Heart of Jesus, glorified by the angels, Heart of Jesus, who didst summon the wise men from afar
Heart of Jesus, the delight of heaven and earth.

Lamb of God, who takest away the sins of the world,
Spare us, O Lord.
Lamb of God, who takest away the sins of the world,
Hear us, O Lord.
Lamb of God, who takest away the sins of the world.
Have mercy on us.

V. Create a clean heart in me, O God,
R. And renew a right spirit within me.

Let us pray .

Almighty God, who by the power of the Holy Ghost didst form the holy and immaculate heart of Jesus, who was born for us in the womb of the blessed Virgin, wit draw from our hearts all worldly inclinations, and make them clean in thy sight, that, serving thee on earth in purity of heart, we may deserve to enjoy the beauty of thy presence for all eternity. Amen.

TUESDAY: Litany of the Sacred Heart of Jesus Conversing Amongst Men

Lord, have mercy on us.
    Christ, have mercy on us.
    Lord, have mercy on us.

Christ, hear us;
    Christ, graciously hear us.

[Respond with: *Have mercy on us.*]
    God the Father of heaven,
    God the Son, Redeemer of the world,
    God the Holy Ghost,
    Holy Trinity, one God,
    Heart of Jesus, conversing amongst men.
    Heart of Jesus, submissive to Mary and Joseph,
    Heart of Jesus, sent by the Father,

Heart of Jesus, led by the Holy Ghost,
Heart of Jesus, full of wisdom,
Heart of Jesus, full of grace and truth,
Heart of Jesus, invincible fortress,
Heart of Jesus, mighty in word and in works.
Heart of Jesus, inflamed with zeal for the glory of God,
Heart of Jesus, severely rebuking the deceitful,
Heart of Jesus, working miracles everywhere,
Heart of Jesus, infinite patience.
Heart of Jesus, refuge of the afflicted.
Heart of Jesus, always solicitous for sinners,
Heart of Jesus, comforter of the afflicted.
Heart of Jesus, immense charity,
Heart of Jesus, full of forbearance for thine enemies,
Heart of Jesus, most faithful to thy friends.
Heart of Jesus, conversing with the pure of heart
Heart of Jesus, model of meekness and humility,
Heart of Jesus, example of all virtues,

Lamb of God, who takest away the sins of the world,
Spare us, O Lord.
Lamb of God, who takest away the sins of the world,
Hear us, O Lord.
Lamb of God, who takest away the sins of the world,
Have mercy upon us.

V. Learn of me, for I am meek and humble of heart,
R. And ye shall find rest to your souls.

Let us pray.
Adorable Jesus! who dwelling on earth didst converse with men,

with a meekness and humility capable of engaging the hearts of all, we beseech thee to increase in us those two sweet virtues which thou dost hold so dear, in order that, following thy example, conversing amongst our brethren with this humility, we may find the rest which thou promisest to the meek and humble of heart, who livest and reignest. Amen.

WEDNESDAY: Litany of the Sacred Heart of Jesus Dwelling in Solitude

Lord, have mercy on us.
   Christ, have mercy on us.
   Lord, have mercy on us.

Jesus, hear us,
   Jesus, graciously hear us.

[Respond with: *Have mercy on us.*]
   God the Father of heaven,
   God the Son, the Redeemer of the world,
   God, the Holy Ghost,
   Holy Trinity, one God,
   Heart of Jesus, solitary,
   Heart of Jesus, enclosed in the womb of Mary,
   Heart of Jesus, reposing in the bosom of the Father,
   Heart of Jesus, lover of solitude,
   Heart of Jesus, heaven of repose,
   Heart of Jesus, always watching over thy elect.
   Heart of Jesus, detached from the world,

Heart of Jesus, passing whole nights in prayer,
Heart of Jesus, absorbed in contemplation.
Heart of Jesus, adoring the Father in spirit and truth,
Heart of Jesus, raised above temptations.
Heart of Jesus, inflamed with love,
Heart of Jesus, mystical cell.
Heart of Jesus, delight of those in solitude,
Heart of Jesus, speaking to the solitary heart,
Heart of Jesus, rendering fruitful the hearts of those who live in retirement,
Heart of Jesus, revealing thy secrets to those living apart from the world,
Heart of Jesus, strength of the solitary,
Heart of Jesus, secure refuge of the solitary,
Heart of Jesus, sweet refreshment of the solitary,
Heart of Jesus, uniting thyself to the solitary heart,
Heart of Jesus, peacefully reigning in the solitary heart,

Lamb of God, who takest away the sins of the world,
Spare us, O Lord.
Lamb of God, who takest away the sins of the world,
Hear us, O Lord.
Lamb of God, who takest away the sins of the world,
Have mercy on us.

V. I will lead the soul into solitude,
  R. And there I will speak to her heart.

Let us pray.
  Adorable Saviour! who didst love solitude, we beseech thee inspire our hearts with the love of retirement, so that, withdrawn from the

tumult of the world, we may hear the sweetness of thy voice in the silence of creatures, and faithfully correspond with the whisperings of the heart and inspirations of thy love, who livest and reignest. Amen.

THURSDAY: Litany of the Sacred Heart of Jesus in the Blessed Sacrament

Lord, have mercy on us.
  Christ, have mercy on us.
  Lord, have mercy on us.

Christ, hear us,
  Christ, graciously hear us.

[Respond with: *Have mercy on us.*]
  God the Father of heaven,
  God the Son, the Redeemer of the world,
  God the Holy Ghost,
  Holy Trinity, one God,
  Heart of Jesus, annihilated in the blessed sacrament,
  Heart of Jesus, inseparably united to that of Mary,
  Heart of Jesus, resplendent Sun of the Church,
  Heart of Jesus, abyss of all virtues,
  Heart of Jesus, good Pastor, lavish of thyself.
  Heart of Jesus, offered up again in sacrifice,
  Heart of Jesus, sacred host,
  Heart of Jesus, consumed for us,
  Heart of Jesus, bond of charity,
  Heart of Jesus, divine seal of our hearts,
  Heart of Jesus, altar of love,

Heart of Jesus, refreshment of holy souls,
Heart of Jesus, adorable feast,
Heart of Jesus, admirable feast.
Heart of Jesus, desirable feast.
Heart of Jesus, delectable feast,
Heart of Jesus, spiritual sweetness tasted in its proper source.
Heart of Jesus, hidden manna,
Heart of Jesus, fountain of living water,
Heart of Jesus, abridgment of the wonders of God,
Heart of Jesus, consuming fire,
Heart of Jesus, source of light.
Heart of Jesus, source of joy,
Heart of Jesus, source of love,
Heart of Jesus, source of all grace,

Lamb of God, who takest away the sins of the world,
Sweet Jesus, Spare us, O Lord.
Lamb of God, who takest away the sins of the world,
Sweet Jesus, Hear us, O Lord.
Lamb of God, who takest away the sins of the world,
Sweet Jesus, Have mercy on us.

V. The heart of Jesus finds its delight
  R. Amongst the children of men.

Let us pray.
  O Jesus, divine lover of mankind, who, in order to gain our hearts and transform them into thine, hast given us, by a marvellous invention of thy love, thine own heart to be our support; we beseech thee, through thy excessive charity, to grant us the grace to receive this sacred bread with such holy dispositions that we may be so happy to return our

hearts for thine, and love for love, who livest and reignest. Amen.

FRIDAY: Litany of the Sacred Heart of Jesus Suffering

Lord, have mercy on us.
    Christ, have mercy on us.
    Lord, have mercy on us.

Jesus, hear us,
    Jesus, graciously hear us.

[Respond with: *Have mercy on us.*]
    God the Father of heaven,
    God the Son, Redeemer of the world,
    God the Holy Ghost, author of all sanctity.
    Holy Trinity, one God,
    Heart of Jesus, suffering,
    Heart of Jesus, sensible to the sorrows of Mary,
    Heart of Jesus, the delight of the eternal Father,
    Heart of Jesus, burning with love for the Cross,
    Heart of Jesus, overwhelmed with bitterness,
    Heart of Jesus, source of contrition,
    Heart of Jesus, seized with fear in the garden.
    Heart of Jesus, sad even unto death,
    Heart of Jesus, betrayed by Judas,
    Heart of Jesus, afflicted by the cowardice of the apostles,
    Heart of Jesus, comforted by an angel,
    Heart of Jesus, weakened even to agony,

Heart of Jesus, submissive to the will of thy Father,
Heart of Jesus, bound by thy love,
Heart of Jesus, suffering every kind of injustice,
Heart of Jesus, abandoned to the fury of man,
Heart of Jesus, torn by the scourges,
Heart of Jesus, pierced by thorns,
Heart of Jesus, pierced with nails,
Heart of Jesus, loaded with indignity,
Heart of Jesus, comfort of the afflicted.
Heart of Jesus, sweet charm of thy servants,
Heart of Jesus, centre of every sorrow,

Lamb of God, who takest away the sins of the world.
Spare us, O Lord.
Lamb of God, who takest away the sins of the world,
Hear us, O Lord.
Lamb of God, who takest away the sins of the world,
Have mercy on us.

V. If we have borne a part in the sufferings of Jesus Christ,
R. We shall have a share in his glory.

Let us pray.

Adorable Saviour, whose sacred heart# full of sorrow and bitterness, has many times bewailed the guilty pleasures of men, we beseech thee, through the infinite merits of thy holy passion, that, making our hearts conformable to thine, we may despise the allurements of the world and the flesh in order to suffer with thee, and deserve through these sufferings to share in thy glory for ever and ever. Amen.

SATURDAY: Litany of the Sacred Heart of Jesus Dying

Lord, have mercy on us.
   Christ, have mercy on us.
   Lord, have mercy on us.

Jesus, hear us,
   Jesus, graciously hear us.

[Respond with: *Have mercy on us.*]
   God the Father of heaven,
   God the Son, Redeemer of the world,
   God the Holy Ghost,
   Holy Trinity, one God,
   Heart of Jesus, dying,
   Heart of Jesus, afflicted by the sadness of Mary,
   Heart of Jesus, the image of the Father,
   Heart of Jesus, obedient onto the death of the Cross,
   Heart of Jesus, victim of expiation,
   Heart of Jesus, freely sacrificed for us,
   Heart of Jesus, breaking on the cross for us.
   Heart of Jesus, wounded on the altar of the cross,
   Heart of Jesus, speaking through a thousand wounds,
   Heart of Jesus, crying by the voice of thy blood,
   Heart of Jesus, disarming divine justice.
   Heart of Jesus, praying for thy enemies.
   Heart of Jesus, thirsting for our salvation.
   Heart of Jesus, exhausted of blood,

Heart of Jesus, sighing of love for us,
Heart of Jesus, dying with love for us,
Heart of Jesus, finishing the work of our redemption.
Heart of Jesus, reconciling heaven with earth.
Heart of Jesus, paradise of crucified souls.
Heart of Jesus, hope of the dying,
Heart of Jesus, throne of mercy,

Lamb of God, who takest away the sins of the world,
Spare us, O Lord.
Lamb of God, who takest away the sins of the world,
Hear us, O Lord,
Lamb of God, who takest away the sins of the world.
Have mercy on us.

V. May my heart expire for love of thee,
R. Since thy heart died for love of me

Let us pray.

O Sovereign Redeemer of mankind, whose heart, raised on the altar of the cross, burned with the sacred fire of charity, vouchsafed to die for us, we beseech thee to inflame our hearts with the fire of the same charity, so that we may have the happiness to aspire only after thee during life, and breathe our last sighs for thee at the hour of death, who livest and reignest world without end. Amen.

SUNDAY: Litany of the Sacred Heart of Jesus Risen from the Dead

Lord, have mercy on us.
>Christ, have mercy on us.
>Lord, have mercy on us.

Jesus, hear us,
>*Jesus, graciously hear us.*

[Respond with: *Have mercy on us.*]
>God the Father of heaven,
>God the Son, Redeemer of the world,
>God the Holy Ghost,
>Holy Trinity, one God,
>Heart of Jesus, risen from the dead,
>Heart of Jesus, the honour and glory of Mary,
>Heart of Jesus, splendour of the Father,
>Heart of Jesus, glorious and triumphant.
>Heart of Jeans, exalted above all hearts,
>Heart of Jesus, the glory of the blessed Trinity,
>Heart of Jesus, placed at the right hand of thy Father,
>Heart of Jesus, full of goodness,
>Heart of Jesus, eternal light,
>Heart of Jesus, friend chosen amongst thousands,
>Heart of Jesus, calling back thy wandering sheep,
>Heart of Jesus, caressing thy apostles,
>Heart of JesuB, wounding the souls of the pure with love,
>Heart of Jesus, visiting thy lovers,
>Heart of Jesus, revealing thy secrets to the pure of heart,

Heart of Jesus, purifying the angels,
Heart of Jesus, sanctifying the archangels,
Heart of Jesus, confirming the thrones.
Heart of Jesus, governing the dominations,
Heart of Jesus, reigning over the principalities,
Heart of Jesus, commanding the powers,
Heart of Jesus, the strength of the virtues.
Heart of Jesus, enlightening the cherubim,
Heart of Jesus, inflaming the seraphim,
Heart of Jesus, the crown of all saints,

Lamb of God, who takest away the sins of the world,
Spare us, O Lord.
Lamb of God, who takest away the sing of the world,
Hear us, O Lord.
Lamb of God, who takest away the sins of the world,
Graciously hear us, O Lord.

V. Thou art the God of my heart,
R. And my portion for all eternity.

Let us pray.

O glorious Redeemer, who art the glory and the happy centre of all hearts, who hast thyself said, that when thou shouldst be raised, thou wouldst draw all things to thyself; we beseech thee, vouchsafe to purify our hearts by the fire of thy divine love, drawing them to thee by the bonds of thy charity, so that they may be transformed into thee, and repose with thee for all eternity, who livest and reignest with God the Father, in the unity of the Holy Ghost, world without end. Amen.

Litany in Honor of the Holy Ghost

Lord, have mercy.
Lord, have mercy.
Christ, have mercy.
Christ, have mercy.
Lord, have mercy.
Lord, have mercy.

Christ, hear us.
Christ graciously hear us,

[Respond with: *Have mercy on us.*]
God the Father, of heaven,
God the Son, Redeemer at the world,
God the Holy Ghost,
Holy Trinity, one God,
Holy Ghost, Who proceedest from the Father and the Son,
Holy Ghost, co-equal with the Father and the Son,
Promise of the Father, most loving and most bounteous,
Gift of the most high God,
Ray of heavenly light,
Author of all good,
Source of living water,

Consuming fire,
Burning love,
Spiritual unction,
Spirit of truth and of power,
Spirit of wisdom and of understanding,
Spirit of counsel and of fortitude,
Spirit of knowledge and of piety,
Spirit of the fear of the Lord,
Spirit of compunction and of penance,
Spirit of grace and of prayer,
Spirit of charity, peace, and joy,
Spirit of patience, longanimity, and goodness,
Spirit of benignity, mildness, and fidelity,
Spirit of modesty, continence, and chastity,
Spirit of the adoption of the sons of God,
Holy Ghost, the comforter,
Holy Ghost, the sanctifier,
Who in the beginning didst move over the waters,
By Whose inspiration spoke the holy men of God,
Who didst overshadow Mary,
Who didst co-operate in the miraculous conception of the Son of God,
Who didst descend upon Him in His baptism,
Who on the day of Pentecost didst appear in fiery tongues upon the disciples of the Lord,
By Whom we also are born again,
Who dwellest in us,
Who governest the Church,
Who fillest the whole world,

LITANY IN HONOR OF THE HOLY GHOST

[Respond with: *We beseech Thee, hear us.*]

Holy Ghost,
That Thou wouldst renew the face of the earth,
That Thou wouldst shed abroad Thy light in our hearts,
That Thou wouldst write Thy law in our hearts,
That Thou wouldst inflame them with the fire of Thy love,
That Thou wouldst open to us the treasures of Thy grace,
That Thou wouldst teach us to ask for them according to Thy will,
That Thou wouldst enlighten us with Thy heavenly inspirations,
That Thou wouldst keep us to Thyself by Thy powerful attractions,
That Thou wouldst grant us the knowledge alone necessary,
That Thou wouldst help us to love and bear with each other,
That Thou wouldst lead us in the way of Thy commandments,
That Thou wouldst make us obedient to Thy inspirations,
That Thou wouldst teach us to pray, and Thyself pray within us,
That Thou wouldst clothe us with love and compassion towards our brethren.
That Thou wouldst inspire us with a horror of evil,
That Thou wouldst direct us in the practice of good,
That Thou wouldst give us the grace of all virtues,
That Thou wouldst cause us to persevere in justice,
That That wouldst be Thy-self our everlasting reward.

Lamb of God, Who takest away the sins of the world,
Spare us, O Lord.
Lamb of God, Who takest away the sins of the world,
Graciously hear us, O Lord.
Lamb of God, Who takest away the sins of the world,
Have mercy on us.

Christ, hear us.
Christ, graciously hear us.

V. Create in us a clean heart, O God.
R. And renew a right spirit within us.

Let us pray

Grant, O merciful Father, that Thy divine spirit may enlighten, inflame, and cleanse our hearts; that He may penetrate us with His heavenly dew, and make us fruitful in good works; through Jesus Christ, our Lord. Amen.

V. The charity of God is poured into our hearts.
R. By the indwelling of His holy Spirit.

Let us pray

May the Holy Ghost, we beseech Thee, O Lrd, inflame us with that fire which Our Lord Jesus Christ came to cast upon the earth, and so earnestly desired that it might be kindled exceedingly; through the same Christ our Lord. Amen.

V. Send forth Thy spirit, and they shall be created.
R. And Thou shalt renew the face of the earth.

Let us pray

O God, Who hast taught the hearts of the faithful by the light of the Holy Spirit; grant that we may, by the gift of the same Spirit, be always truly wise, and ever rejoice in His consolations; through Christ our Lord. Amen.

Litany of the Holy Ghost for Pentecost

Lord, have mercy on us.
> Lord, have mercy on us.
> Christ, have mercy on us.
> Christ, have mercy on us.
> Lord, have mercy on us.
> Lord, have mercy on us.

Christ, hear us.
> Christ, graciously hear us.

God, the Father of heaven,
> Have mercy on us.
> God, the Son, Redeemer of the world,
> Have mercy on us.
> God, the Holy Ghost,
> Have mercy on us.
> Holy Trinity, one God,
> Have mercy on us.

[Hymn]
> Come, Holy Ghost, send down those beams
> Which sweetly flow in silent streams

From Thy bright throne above.

Come Thou the Father of the poor,
   Thou bounteous source of all our store,
   Come, fire our hearts with love.

Come, Thou of comforters the best;
   Come, Thou the soul's delicious guest,
   The pilgrim's sweet relief.

Thou art our rest in toil and sweat,
   Refreshment heat, in excessive
   And solace in our grief,

O sacred light, shoot home Thy darts;
   Oh, pierce the center of these hearts
   Whose faith aspires to Thee.

Without Thy Godhead nothing can
   Have any price or worth in man,
   Nothing can harmless be.

Lord, wash our sinful stains away;
   Water from heaven our barren clay;
   Our wounds and bruises heal.

To Thy sweet yoke our stiff necks bow;
   Warm with Thy fire our hearts of snow;
   Our wandering feet repeal,

LITANY OF THE HOLY GHOST FOR PENTECOST

O grant Thy faithful, dearest Lord,
  Whose only hope is Thy sure word,
  The seven gifts of Thy Spirit.

Grant us in life to obey Thy grace;
  Grant us at death to see Thy face;
  And endless joys inherit.

[Respond with: *We beseech Thee, hear us.*]
O God, we beseech Thee, send the Holy Spirit into our hearts; and by His sacred presence and power, may He banish from thence the spirit of the world, and of a disorderly life.
  The spirit of sloth, of self-love, and of the love of ease.
  The spirit of hatred and contention,
  The spirit of intemperance and impurity,
  The spirit of pride and vanity,
  The spirit of envy and contention.
  The spirit of detraction, calumny, and uncharitableness,
  The spirit of dissembling, flattering, and lying,
  The spirit of revenge, passion, and impatience,
  The spirit of incredulity and profaneness,
  The spirit of immoderate solicitude and worldly care,
  The spirit of tepidity and impiety,
  The spirit of prodigality and covetousness,
  The spirit of frivolity and inconstancy,
  And may He give us the spirit of universal charity, by which we may love God above all things, and our neighbors as ourselves,

Lamb of God, Who takest away the sins of the world,
  Spare us, O Lord.
  Lamb of God, Who takest away the sins of the world,

Hear us, O Lord.
Lamb of God, Who takest away the sins of the world,
Have mercy on us.

V. Create in us a clean heart, O God.
  R. And renew a right spirit within us.
  V. Send forth Thy spirit and they shall be created.
  R. And Thou shalt renew the face of the earth.

Let us pray

O God Who hast taught the hearts of the faithful by the light of the Holy Spirit; grant that, by the gift of the same Spirit, we may be always truly wise, and ever rejoice in His consolations. Through Christ, our Lord. Amen.

Litany of the Love of God

Composed by Pope Pius VI

Lord, have mercy on us.
Lord, have mercy on us.
Christ, have mercy on us.
Christ, have mercy on us.
Lord, have mercy on us.
Lord, have mercy on us.

Christ, hear us.
Christ, graciously hear us.

God, the Father of heaven,
Have mercy on us.
God, the Son, Redeemer of the world,
Have mercy on us.
God, the Holy Ghost,
Have mercy on us.
Holy Trinity, one God,
Have mercy on us.

[Respond with: *I love Thee, O my God.*]

Thou Who art infinite love,
Thou Who didst first love me,
Thou Who commandest me to love Thee,
With all my heart,
With all my soul,
With all my mind,
With all my strength,
Above all possessions and honors,
Above all pleasures and enjoyments,
More than myself, and me, everything belonging to me,
More than all my relatives and friends,
More than all men and angels,
Above all created things in heaven or on earth,
Only for Thyself,
Because Thou art the sovereign good,
Because Thou art infinitely worthy of being loved,
Because Thou art infinitely perfect,
Even hadst Thou not promised me heaven,
Even hadst Thou not menaced me with hell,
Even shouldst Thou try me by want and misfortune,
In wealth and in poverty,
In prosperity and in adversity,
In health and in sickness,
In life and in death,
In time and in eternity,
In union with that love wherewith all the saints and all the angels love Thee in heaven,
In union with that love wherewith the Blessed Virgin Mary loveth Thee,
In union with that infinite love wherewith Thou lovest Thyself eternally.

Let us pray

My God, Who dost possess in incomprehensible abundance all that is perfect and worthy of love! Annihilate in me all guilty, sensual, and undue love of creatures, kindle in my heart the pure fire of Thy love, so that I may love nothing but Thee, or in Thee, until, being entirely consumed by holy love of Thee, I may go to love Thee eternally with the elect in heaven, the home of pure love. Amen.

O God, Who hast prepared all good things for them that love Thee! Pour into our hearts such a desire of Thy love, that we, loving Thee in all and above all, may attain to the realization of Thy heavenly promises, which exceed all that we can desire. Through Christ our Lord. Amen.

Litany of Glory

Lord, receive our praise.
   Christ, receive our praise.
   Christ, receive our adoration.
   Christ, graciously receive our adoration.

God the Father of heaven.
   Salvation and power and glory to our God.
   God the Son, Redeemer of the world.
   Salvation and power and glory to our God,
   God the Holy Ghost.
   Salvation and power and glory to our God,
   Holy Trinity, one God.
   Salvation and power and glory to our God,

Holy holy, holy. Lord God Almighty,
   Who was and who is, and who is to come.

[Respond with: *Glory to God alone.*]
   Sing to the Lord a new canticle: sing to the Lord all the earth.
   Sing ye to the Lord, and bless his name: shew forth his salvation from day to day.
   Declare his glory among the Gentiles: his wonders amongst all

people.

For who is God save the Lord ? or who is salvation but our God; — God, who hath girded me with strength, and made my way blameless?

For thou hast maintained my right and my cause; thou hast sat on the throne judging justice.

The ways of the Lord are good; the words of the Lord are sure; he is a shield to all who trust in him.

Thou hast multiplied thy mercy, O God; the children of men shall put their trust under the shadow of thy wing.

I will give glory to God according to his rignteousness; and I will sing praise to the name of the Lord the most high.

I will give praise to thee, O Lord, with my whole heart: I will tell all thy wonders.

The Lord is most high, he is terrible; he is a great king over all the earth.

Thou hast put on praise and beauty; thou art clothed with light as with a garment; thou stretchest out the heavens like a pavilion; thou makest the clouds thy chariot; thou walkest upon the wings of the wind.

The voice of the Lord is upon the waters; the God of majesty speaketh in the thunder; the voice of the Lord is power; the voice of the Lord is majesty.

The Lord ruleth the floods: the Lord is king for ever.

The Lord shall reign to eternity; yea, for ever and ever.

Let all that seek thee rejoice and be glad in thee: let such as love thy salvation say always. The Lord be magnified.

Who is the King of Glory? the Lord of hosts, he is the King of Glory.

How manifold are thy works, O Lord! thou hast made all things in wisdom. The earth is filled with thy riches.

For thou hast given me, O Lord, a delight in thy works and in the works of thy hands I shall rejoice.

Thou hast made known to me the ways of life and thou shalt cheer me with the fulness of joy, with thee are delights for evermore.

I will love thee, O Lord, my strength. The Lord is my strength, my refuge, and my deliverer; my God, my helper in whom I will trust; my protector, my stay, and the giver of my salvation.

The Lord is my shepherd, I shall not want; he hath set me in pastures of tender grass, beside gently-running waters. He hath strengthened my soul and brought me on the paths of righteousness for his name's sake.

Thy goodness and mercy shall follow me all the days of my life: and. I shall dwell in the house of the Lord unto length of days.

Blessed be the Lord, day by day; the God of my salvation will make our journey prosperous to us.

God is the king of all the earth; sing ye his praise gladly.

Sing praises to the Lord, sing ye: sing praise to the Lord, sing ye.

Let every spirit praise the Lord: praise ye the Lord.

I will sing to the Lord as long as I live : I will sing praises to the Lord while I have any being.

Turn, O my soul, to thy rest; for the Lord hath dealt bountifully to thee.
Glory to God alone

Lamb of God, who wast slain, and hast redeemed us with thy blood. Benediction, and honour, and power for ever and ever.

Lamb of God, who wast slain, and hast redeemed us with thy blood. Benediction, and honour, and power, for ever and ever.

Lamb of God, who wast slain, and hast redeemed us with thy blood. Benediction, and honour, and power, for ever and ever.

Glory be to the Father, Son, and Holy Ghost; as it was in the beginning, is now, and ever shall be, world without end.

Accept, most great and glorious King, the offering of our praise. Teach us not only to glorify thee; but to glorify thee alone. Teach us to renounce ourselves and our own perverse gratifications ; and truly to do all things for the glory of God. Let us ever remember the many blessings we have received from thee. Let us ever remember that thou hast created us; that thou hast redeemed us; that thou hast called us to thyself; and hast given us the means of salvation. Often hast thou heard our prayers, O Lord: often hast thou granted our requests; and, more often still hast thou upheld and protected us in thine own mercy when we had neither the grace to call for thine assistance nor to acknowledge thy goodness

To thee, O Lord, be glory;
To thee be praise and thanksgiving.

Glory be to the Father, Son, and Holy Ghost:
As it was in the beginning is now, and ever shall be, world without end. Amen.

III

Litanies to the Blessed Virgin Mary

Litany of the Dolors of the Blessed Virgin Mary

Lord have mercy.
Lord have mercy.
Christ have mercy.
Christ have mercy.
Lord have mercy.
Lord have mercy.

Christ hear us.
Christ graciously hear us.

[Respond with: *Have mercy on us.*]
God the Father of heaven,
God the Son, Redeemer of the world,
God the Holy Ghost,
Holy Trinity, one God,

[Respond with: *Pray for us.*]
Mother of dolours,
Thou who didst find no room in the inn,
Who wast forced to take refuge in a stable,
Who didst lay thy First-born in a manger,

Who didst witness with compassion the Circumcision of thy Son,

Who didst hear that thy Son was set as a sign that should be contradicted,

Who didst hear that thine own soul should be pierced with a sword,

Who wast fain to fly into Egypt with thy Son,

Who didst grieve for the murder of the Innocents,

Who for three days didst seek sorrowing thy Son, lost in the Temple, when he was twelve years old,

Who didst painfully note the constant hatred of the Jews against Him,

Who, on the day of the Last Supper, didst bid a sad farewell to thy Son going to Jerusalem to suffer.

Who didst learn that He was betrayed by Judas, and led away captive.

Who didst see Him delivered up as a malefactor to the chief priests.

Who didst hear that He was falsely accused.

Who didst learn that His blessed face was struck with a fearful blow.

Who didst hear that He was most cruelly treated by the Jews and by the soldiers,

Who didst hear thy Son rejected for Barabbas,

Who didst behold Him beaten with scourges and crowned with thorns.

Who didst hear the unjust sentence pronounced against Him,

Who didst go to meet thy Son loaded with the weight of the Cross,

Who didst hear His blessed hands and feet being pierced with dreadful nails,

Who didst receive the last words of thy Son upon the Cross,

Who didst stand by Him in his agony,

Who didst receive into thy maternal bosom the lifeless body of thy Son, taken down from the Cross,

Who, after the body of thy Son was buried, didst return home all sad and desolate,

O Queen of martyrs,

O Mirror of the afflicted,
O Comfort of the weak,
O Strength of the fearful,
O Refuge of sinners,

[Respond with: *Deliver us, O Queen of Martyrs.*]
Through the most bitter Passion and Death of thy Son,
Through the most poignant sorrows of thy heart,
Through thy exceeding sadness and Desolation,
Through thy extreme anguish,
Through thy groans and tears,
Through thy maternal compassion,
Through thy most powerful patronage,
From immoderate sadness,
From a pusillanimous spirit,
From every occasion and danger of sin,
From the snares of the devil
From hardness of heart,
From impenitence,
From sudden and unprepared-for death.
From eternal damnation.

We sinners,
Beseech thee, hear us.

[Respond with: *We beseech thee, hear us.*]
That thou wouldst vouchsafe to preserve us by thy patronage in true faith, hope, and charity,
That thou wouldst vouchsafe to obtain for us from thy Son perfect sorrow and repentance for our sins,
That thou wouldst vouchsafe to bring consolation and assistance to

those who call upon thee,
>   That thou wouldst vouchsafe to succour us in the agony of death,
>   That thou wouldst vouchsafe to obtain for us a happy end,
>   Mother of God,

Lamb of God, who takest away the sins of the world,
>   *Spare us, O Lord.*
>   Lamb of God, who takest away the sins of the world,
>   *Graciously hear us, O Lord.*
>   Lamb of God, who takest away the sins of the world.
>   *Have mercy on us.*

Christ hear us.
>   *Christ graciously hear us.*

Lord have mercy.
>   Christ have mercy.
>   Lord have mercy.

V. In all our tribulations and afflictions,
>   **R**. Succour us, O most blessed Virgin Mary.

Let us pray.

O Lord Jesus Christ, grant, we beseech thee, that the blessed Virgin Mary thy Mother, whose most sacred soul was pierced with the sword of sorrow in the hour of thy Passion, may intercede for us with thy mercy, now and at the hour of our death, through thine own merits, O Jesus, Saviour of die world. Who, with the Father and the Holy Ghost, livest and reignest, God, world without end. Amen.

Litany of the Holy Name of Mary

Lord have mercy.
> *Lord have mercy.*
> Christ have mercy.
> *Christ have mercy.*
> Lord have mercy.
> *Lord have mercy.*

Son of Mary, hear us.
> *Son of Mary, graciously hear us.*

[Respond with: *Have mercy on us.*]
> Heavenly Father, of whom Mary is the Daughter,
> Eternal Word, of whom Mary is the Mother,
> Holy Spirit, of whom Mary is the Spouse,
> Divine Trinity, of whom Mary is the Handmaid,

[Respond with: *Pray for us.*]
> Mary, Mother of the Living God,
> Mary, Daughter of the Light Eternal,
> Mary, our light,
> Mary, our sister,
> Mary, flower of Jesse,

Mary, issue of kings,
Mary, chief work of God,
Mary, the beloved of God,
Mary, immaculate virgin,
Mary, all fair,
Mary, light in darkness,
Mary, our sure rest,
Mary, house of God,
Mary, sanctuary of the Lord,
Mary, altar of the Divinity,
Mary, Virgin Mother,
Mary, embracing thy Infant God,
Mary, reposing with Eternal Wisdom,
Mary, ocean of bitterness,
Mary, suffering with thy only Son,
Mary, pierced with a sword of sorrow,
Mary, torn with a cruel wound,
Mary, sorrowful even to death,
Mary, bereft of all consolation,
Mary, submissive to the law of God,
Mary, standing by the cross of Jesus,
Mary, our lady,
Mary, our queen.
Mary, queen of glory,
Mary, glory of the Church triumphant,
Mary, blessed queen,
Mary, advocate of the Church militant,
Mary, queen of mercy,
Mary, consoler of the Church suffering,
Mary, exalted above the Angels,
Mary, crowned with twelve stars,

LITANY OF THE HOLY NAME OF MARY

Mary, fair as the moon,
Mary, bright as the sun,
Mary, distinguished above
Mary, seated at the right hand of Jesus,
Mary, our hope,
Mary, our sweetness,
Mary, glory of Jerusalem, Mary, joy of Israel,
Mary, honour of our people,
Mary, our Lady of the Immaculate Conception,
Mary, our Lady of the Assumption,
Mary, our Lady of Dolours,
Mary, our Lady of Mercy,
Mary, our Lady, Star of the sea,
Mary, our Lady of the Rosary,
Mary, our Lady of Victory,
Mary, our Lady of La Trappe,
Mary, our Lady of Mount Carmel,

Lamb of God, who didst rejoice Mary,
Spare us, O Lord Jesus.
Lamb of God, who didst afflict Mary,
Graciously hear us, O Lord Jesus.
Lamb of God, who didst glorify Mary,
Have mercy on us, O Lord Jesus.

Son of Mary, hear us.
Son of Mary, graciously hear us.

V. I will declare thy name unto my brethren.
   R. I will praise thee in the assembly of the faithful.

Let us pray.

O Almighty God, who beholdest thy servants earnestly desirous to place themselves under the shadow of the name and protection of the most holy Virgin Mary; vouchsafe, we beseech thee, that, by her charitable intercession, we may be delivered from all evil on earth, and may arrive at everlasting joys in heaven. Through Jesus Christ our Lord. Amen.

Litany of the Immaculate Conception

Lord have mercy.
Lord have mercy.
Christ have mercy.
Christ have mercy.
Lord have mercy.
Lord have mercy.
Christ hear us.
Christ, graciously hear us.

God the Father, Source of all sanctity,
Have mercy on us.
God the Son, increated Sanctity,
Have mercy on us.
God the Holy Ghost, Spirit of sanctity,
Have mercy on us.
Most sacred Trinity, one God,
Have mercy on us.

[Respond: *Pray for us.*]
Holy Mary, immaculate,
Holy Virgin, by predestination immaculate,
Holy Virgin, in thy conception immaculate,

Holy Virgin, after thy conception immaculate,
Daughter of the Father, immaculate,
Mother of the Son, immaculate,
Spouse of the Holy Ghost, immaculate,
Seat of the most holy Trinity, immaculate,
Image of the Wisdom of God, immaculate,
Dawn of the Sun of Justice, immaculate,
Living Ark of the body of Christ, immaculate,
Daughter of David, immaculate,
Guide to Jesus, immaculate,
Virgin triumphing over original sin, immaculate,
Virgin, crushing the head of the serpent, immaculate,
Queen of heaven and earth, immaculate,
Gate of the heavenly Jerusalem, immaculate,
Dispenser of graces, immaculate,
Spouse of St. Joseph, immaculate,
Star of the world, immaculate,
Impregnable tower of the Church militant, immaculate,
Rose amid thorns, immaculate,
Olive of the fields, immaculate,
Model of all perfection, immaculate,
Cause of our hope, immaculate,
Pillar of our faith, immaculate,
Source of divine love, immaculate,
Sure sign of our salvation, immaculate,
Rule of perfect obedience, immaculate,
Pattern of holy poverty, immaculate,
School of devotion, immaculate,
Abode of chaste modesty, immaculate,
Anchor of our salvation, immaculate,
Light of Angels, immaculate,

LITANY OF THE IMMACULATE CONCEPTION

Crown of Patriarchs, immaculate,
Glory of Prophets, immaculate,
Lady and Mistress of Apostles, immaculate,
Support of Martyrs, immaculate,
Strength of Confessors, immaculate,
Diadem of Virgins, immaculate,
Splendor of all Saints, immaculate,
Sanctity of all Christians, immaculate,
Companion of devout souls, immaculate,
Joy of those who hope in thee, immaculate,
Health of the sick, immaculate,
Advocate of sinners, immaculate,
Terror of heretics, immaculate,
Protectress of all mankind, immaculate,
Patroness of those who honor thee, immaculate,

Lamb of God, who takes away the sins of the world,
Spare us, O Lord.
Lamb of God, who takes away the sins of the world,
Graciously hear us, O Lord.
Lamb of God, who takes away the sins of the world,
Have mercy on us.

V. In thy conception, O Virgin Mary, then was immaculate.
R. Pray for us to the Father, whose son Jesus, conceived of the Holy Ghost, thou did bring forth.

Let us Pray:
O Almighty and Eternal God, who didst prepare for thy Son a worthy habitation, by the immaculate conception of the blessed Virgin Mary; we beseech thee, that, as thou didst preserve her from every stain of

sin, through the merits of the pre-ordained atonement of Jesus Christ, so thou wouldst grant, that we also may come without spot to thee. Through the same Jesus Christ our Lord.

    Amen.

Litany of Our Lady of Sorrows

Lord have mercy.
   Lord have mercy.
Christ have mercy.
   Christ have mercy.
Lord have mercy.
   Lord have mercy.

Christ hear us.
   Christ graciously hear us.

God the Father of heaven,
   God the Son, Redeemer of the world,
   God the Holy Ghost,
   Holy Trinity, one God,

[Respond with: *Pray for us.*]
   Holy Mary,
   Holy Mother of God,
   Holy Virgin of virgins,
   Mother crucified,
   Mother sorrowful,
   Mother tearful,

Mother afflicted,
Mother forsaken,
Mother desolate,
Mother bereft of thy child,
Mother transfixed with the sword,
Mother consumed with grief,
Mother filled with anguish,
Mother crucified in heart,
Mother most sad,
Fountain of tears,
Mass of suffering,
Mirror of patience,
Rock of constancy,
Anchor of confidence,
Refuge of the forsaken,
Shield of the oppressed,
Subduer of the unbelieving,
Comfort of the wretched,
Medicine of the sick,
Strength of the weak,
Harbour of the wrecked,
Allayer of tempests,
Resource of mourners,
Terror of the treacherous,
Treasure of the faithful,
Eye of Prophets,
Staff of Apostles,
Crown of Martyrs,
Light of Confessors,
Pearl of Virgins,
Consolation of Widows,

Joy of all Saints,

Lamb of God, who takest away the sins of the world,
Spare us, O Jesus.
Lamb of God, who takest away the sins of the world,
Graciously hear us, O Jesus.
Lamb of God, who takest away the sins of the world.
Have mercy on us, O Jesus.

Let us pray.
   Look down upon us, deliver us from all trouble in the power of Jesus Christ. Amen.

Imprint, O Lady, thy wounds upon my heart, that I may read therein sorrow and love: sorrow, to endure every sorrow for thee; love, to despise every love for thee.

Credo. Salve regina. Three Ave Marias, in honour of the most holy heart of Mary.

Litany of the Life of the Blessed Virgin Mary

Lord have mercy.
  Lord have mercy.
  Christ have mercy.
  Christ have mercy.
  Lord have mercy.
  Lord have mercy.

Christ hear us.
  Christ graciously hear us.

[Respond with: *Have mercy on us.*]
  God the Father of heaven,
  God the Son, Redeemer of the world,
  God the Holy Ghost,
  Holy Trinity, one God,

[Respond with: *Pray for us.*]
  Holy Mary,
  Holy Virgin, sprung from the race of David,
  Holy Virgin, espoused to the just Joseph,
  Holy Virgin, bound by an inviolable vow of chastity,

LITANY OF THE LIFE OF THE BLESSED VIRGIN MARY

Holy Virgin, gloriously saluted by the Angel,
Holy Virgin, full of grace,
Holy Virgin, blessed among all women,
Holy Virgin, conceiving by the operation of the Holy Ghost,
Holy Virgin, bearing in thy womb the Man-God,
Holy Virgin, Mother of the Lord,
Holy Virgin, Mother of the true Solomon,
Holy Virgin, visiting thy cousin Elizabeth,
Holy Virgin, blest land, whence sprung the Saviour,
Holy Virgin, holy gate, through which the King of heaven alone may pass,
Holy Virgin, journeying to Bethlehem with thy spouse Joseph,
Holy Virgin, bringing into the world thy divine Son,
Holy Virgin, laying the Son of God in a manger,
Holy Virgin, visited by the shepherds.
Holy Virgin, saluted by the magi,
Holy Virgin, presenting thy Son to be circumcised.
Holy Virgin, submitting to the law of purification,
Holy Virgin, offering thy dear Son in the temple,
Holy Virgin, flying into Egypt to save thy Child,
Holy Virgin, returning from Egypt into the land of Israel,
Holy Virgin, leading an obscure life at Nazareth,
Holy Virgin, keeping the feasts prescribed by the law,
Holy Virgin, afflicted at the loss of thy Child, when he was twelve years old,
Holy Virgin, seeking thy child for three days sorrowing,
Holy Virgin, honouring with thy presence the marriage-feast of Cana,
Holy Virgin, graciously representing to thy Son the want of wine,
Holy Virgin, obtaining a miracle by thy intercession,
Holy Virgin, following thy Son in his ministrations,
Holy Virgin, sharing the sorrows of thy Son,

Holy Virgin, standing at the foot of the cross,
Holy Virgin, confided by thy Son to the beloved disciple,
Holy Virgin, pierced with a sword of sorrow,
Holy Virgin, filled with the Holy Spirit on the day of Pentecost,
Holy Virgin, called Blessed by all generations,
Holy Virgin, reigning in heaven,

Lamb of God, who takest away the sins of the world,
Spare us, O Lord.
Lamb of God, who takest away the sins of the world,
Graciously hear us, O Lord.
Lamb of God, who takest away the sins of the world.
Have mercy on us.

V. Pray for us, O holy Mother of God.
R. That we may be made worthy of the promises of Christ.

Let us pray.

Protect, O Lord, thy servants by thy gracious and abundant help and grant that our confidence in the protection of the Blessed Mary ever virgin may obtain for us security against all enemies and all dangers. Through our Lord Jesus Christ. Amen

Litany of the Sacred Heart of Mary

Lord have mercy.
Lord have mercy.
Christ have mercy.
Christ have mercy.
Lord have mercy.
Lord have mercy.

Christ hear us.
Christ graciously hear us.

[Respond with: *Have mercy on us.*]
God the Father of heaven,
God the Son, Redeemer of the world,
God the Holy Ghost,
Holy Trinity, one God,

[Respond with: *Pray for us.*]
Heart of Mary,
Heart of Mary, according to the Heart of God,
Heart of Mary, united to the Heart of Jesus,
Heart of Mary, organ of the Holy Ghost,
Heart of Mary, sanctuary of the Divine Trinity,

Heart of Mary, tabernacle of God incarnate,
Heart of Mary, immaculate from thy creation,
Heart of Mary, full of grace,
Heart of Mary, blessed among all hearts,
Heart of Mary, throne of glory,
Heart of Mary, abyss of humility,
Heart of Mary, holocaust of divine lore,
Heart of Mary, fastened to g the cross with Jesus crucified,
Heart of Mary, comfort of the afflicted,
Heart of Mary, refuge of sinners,
Heart of Mary, hope of the agonising,
Heart of Mary, seat of mercy,

Lamb of God, who takest away the sins of the world,
Spare us, O Lord .
Lamb of God, who takest away the sins of the world,
Graciously hear us, O Lord.
Lamb of God, who takest away the sins of the world.
Have mercy on us.

Christ hear us.
Christ graciously hear us,

V. Immaculate Mary, meek and humble of heart.
R. Make our heart according to the Heart of Jesus.

Let us pray.
O most merciful God, who, for the salvation of sinners and the refuge of the miserable, wast pleased that the Immaculate Heart of the blessed Virgin Mary should be most like in charity and pity to the Divine Heart of thy Son Jesus Christ; grant that we, who commemorate this most

sweet and loving Heart, may, by the merits and intercession of the same blessed Virgin, merit to be found according to the Heart of Jesus. Through the same Christ our Lord. Amen.

IV

Litanies in Honor of the Various Saints

Litany of St. Aloysius

Lord have mercy.
   Lord have mercy.
Christ have mercy.
   Christ have mercy.
Lord have mercy.
   Lord have mercy.

Christ hear us.
   Christ graciously hear us.

God the Father of heaven,
   Have mercy on us.
God the Son, Redeemer of the world,
   Have mercy on us.
God the Holy Ghost,
   Have mercy on us.
Holy Trinity, one God,
   Have mercy on us.

[Respond: *Pray for us.*]
   Holy Mary,
   Holy Mother of God,

Holy Virgin of Virgins,
St. Aloysius,
Most beloved of Christ,
The delight of the Blessed Virgin,
Most chaste youth,
Angelic youth,
Most humble youth,
Model of young students,
Despiser of riches,
Enemy of vanities,
Scorner of honors,
Honor of princes
Jewel of the nobility,
Flower of innocence,
Ornament of a religious state,
Mirror of mortification,
Mirror of perfect obedience,
Lover of evangelical poverty,
Most affectionately devout,
Most zealous observer of rules,
Most desirous of the salvation of souls,
Perpetual adorer of the holy Eucharist,
Particular client of St. Ignatius,
[Respond: *Be merciful, hear us, O Lord.*]
Be merciful spare us, O Lord.
From the concupiscence of the eyes,
From the concupiscence of the flesh,
From the pride of life,
Through the merits and intercession of Aloysius,
Through his angelical purity,
Through his sanctity and glory,

We sinners,
Beseech thee hear us.

Lamb of God, who takes away the sins of the world,
Spare us O Lord.

Lamb of God, who takes away the sins of the world,
Hear us, O Lord.

Lamb of God, who takes away the sins of the world,
Have mercy on us.

Christ, bear us.
Christ, graciously hear us.

V. Pray for us, St. Aloysius.
R. That we may be made worthy of the promises of Christ.

Let us Pray.

O God! the distributor of heavenly gifts, who did unite in the angelic youth Aloysius, wonderful innocence of life with an equal severity of penance, grant through his merits and prayers that we, who have not followed the example of his innocence, may imitate his practice of penance; through our Lord Jesus Christ.

Amen.

Litany of St. Anne

Lord have mercy.
Lord have mercy.
Christ have mercy.
Christ have mercy.
Lord have mercy.
Lord have mercy.

Christ hear us.
Christ graciously hear us.

[Respond with: *Have mercy on us.*]
God the Father of heaven,
God the Son, Redeemer of the world,
God the Holy Ghost,
Holy Trinity, one God,

[Respond with: *Pray for us.*]
St. Anne,
St. Anne, mother of the Virgin Mary,
St. Anne, spouse of Joachim,
St. Anne, mother-in-law of Joseph,
St. Anne, ark of Noah,

St. Anne, ark of the covenant,
St. Anne, mount Horeb,
St. Anne, rod of Jesse,
St. Anne, fruitful tree,
St. Anne, fruit-bearing vine,
St. Anne, sprung from the blood of kings,
St. Anne, joy of Angels,
St. Anne, grace of Patriarchs,
St. Anne, oracle of Prophets,
St. Anne, praise of all Saints,
St. Anne, glory of Priests and Levites,
St. Anne, cloud full of dew,
St. Anne, cloud of light,
St. Anne, cloud of brightness,
St. Anne, vessel full of grace,
St. Anne, mirror of obedience,
St. Anne, mirror of patience,
St. Anne, mirror of compassion,
St. Anne, mirror of devotion,
St. Anne, bulwark of the Church,
St. Anne, refuge of sinners,
St. Anne, protectress of Christians,
St. Anne, deliverer of captives,
St. Anne, consolation of the married,
St. Anne, mother of widows,
St. Anne, directress of virgins,
St. Anne, harbour of safety for voyagers,
St. Anne, sure road for travellers,
St. Anne, support of the weak,
St. Anne, health of the sick,
St. Anne, light of the blind,

St. Anne, tongue of the dumb,
St. Anne, ear of the deaf,
St. Anne, comforter of the afflicted,
St. Anne, succour of all those who call upon thee.

Lamb of God, who takest away the sins of the world.
Spare us , O Lord.
Lamb of God, who takest awai the sins of the world.
Graciously hear us, O Lord.
Lamb of God, who takest away the sins of the world.
Have mercy on us.

Christ Jesus, hear us.
Christ Jesus, graciously hear us.

V. Pray for us, St. Anne.
R. That we may be made worthy of the promises of Christ.

Let us pray

O almighty and eternal God, who didst vouchsafe to choose St. Anne to bring into the world the Mother of thy only Son; mercifully grant to us, we beseech thee, who devoutly honor her memory, grace to obtain, through her merits, the blessings of eternal life. Who livest and reignest, world without end. Amen.

Litany of Blessed Julia Billart

(Foundress of the Congregation, Sisters of Notre Dame)

Lord, have mercy on us.
   Christ, have mercy on us.
   Lord, have mercy on us.
   Christ, hear us.
   Christ, graciously hear us.

[Respond with: *Have mercy on us.*]
   God, the Father of heaven,
   God the Son, Redeemer of the world,
   God, the Holy Ghost,
   Holy Trinity, one God,

[Respond with: *Pray for us.*]
   Holy Mary, Mother of God.
   Saint Joseph.
   Blessed Julia.
   Blessed Julia, faithful disciple of the Heart of Jesus.
   Blessed Julia, miraculously cured by the Heart of Jesus.
   Blessed Julia, devoted to the glory of the Heart of Jesus.
   Blessed Julia, lover of the Heart of Jesus.

Blessed Julia, whose habitual dwelling was the Heart of Jesus, pray for us.

Blessed Julia, whose Institute had its birth in the Heart of Jesus.

V. Blessed Julia, powerful over the Heart of Jesus,
R. Intercede for us that this Divine Heart may grant our request.

Let us pray

O God, Who didst give to Blessed Julia constant courage to overcome all the obstacles she encountered in the execution of Thy holy will, may it please Thee to grant that all who, with confidence, claim her protection with Thee, may feel the effects of her intercession, and obtain their just requests from Thy infinite bounty, Who livest and reignest, etc. Amen.

Litany of the Holy Angels

Lord have mercy.
Lord have mercy.
Christ have mercy.
Christ have mercy.
Lord have mercy.
Lord have mercy.

Christ hear us.
Christ graciously hear us.

[Respond with: *Have mercy on us.*]
   God the Father of heaven,
   God the Son, Redeemer of the world,
   God the Holy Ghost,
   Holy Trinity, one God,

[Respond with: *Pray for us.*]
   Holy Mary, Queen of Angels,
   Holy Mother of God,
   Holy Virgin of virgins,
   St. Michael, who wast ever the defender of the people of God,
   St. Michael, who didst drive from heaven Lucifer and his rebel crew,

St. Michael, who didst cast a down to hell the accuser of our brethren,

St. Gabriel, who didst expound to Daniel the heavenly vision,

St. Gabriel, who didst foretell to Zachary the birth and ministry of John the Baptist,

St. Gabriel, who didst announce to Mary the Incarnation of the Divine Word,

St. Raphael, who didst lead Tobias safe through his journey to his home again,

St. Raphael, who didst deliver Sara from the devil, St. Raphael, who didst restore his sight to Tobias the elder.

All ye holy Angels, who stand upon the high and lofty throne of God,

Who cry to him continually, Holy, holy, holy.

Who dispel the darkness of our minds, and give us light.

Who are the messengers of heavenly things to men,

Who have been appointed by God to be our guardians.

Who always behold the face of our Father who is in heaven,

Who rejoice over one sinner doing penance.

Who struck the Sodomites with blindness.

Who led Lot out of the midst of the ungodly.

Who ascended and descended on the ladder of Jacob,

Who delivered the divine law to Moses on mount Sinai

Who brought good tidings when Christ was born,

Who ministered to Him in the desert.

Who comforted Him in his agony.

Who sat in white garments at His sepulchre,

Who appeared to the disciples as He went up into heaven,

Who shall go before Him bearing the standard of the Cross, when He cometh to judgment,

Who shall gather together the elect at the end of the world,

Who shall separate the wicked from among the just.

Who offer to God the prays of them that pray,

LITANY OF THE HOLY ANGELS

Who assist us at the hour of death,
Who carried Lazarus into Abraham's bosom,
Who conduct to heaven the souls of the just, cleansed from every stain,
Who perform signs and wonders by the power of God,
Who are sent to minister for those who shall receive the inheritance of salvation,
Who would cure Babylon, and when she will not be cured, depart and forsake her,
Who are set over kingdoms and provinces,
Who Have often put to flight armies of enemies,
Who have often delivered God's servants from prison, and other perils of this life,
Who have often consoled the holy Martyrs in their torments,
Who are wont to cherish with peculiar care the prelates and princes of the Church, and all that are under their charge,
All ye holy orders of blessed Spirits,

[Respond with: *Deliver us, O Lord, by thy holy Angels.*]
From all dangers,
From the snares of the devil,
From all heresy and schism,
From plague, famine, and war,
From sudden and unlooked for death,
From everlasting death,

We sinners,
Beseech thee, hear us.

[Respond with: *We beseech Thee, hear us.*]
Through thy holy Angels,

That thou wouldst spare us,
That thou wouldst pardon us,
That thou wouldst vouchsafe to govern and preserve thy holy Church,
That thou wouldst vouchsafe to protect our Apostolic Prelate, and all ecclesiastical orders,
That thou wouldst vouchsafe to grant peace and security to kings and all Christian princes,
That thou wouldst vouchsafe to give and preserve the fruits of the earth,
That thou wouldst vouchsafe to grant eternal rest to all the faithful departed,

Lamb of God, who takest away the sins of the world,
Spare us, O Lord.
Lamb of God, who takest away the sins of the world
Graciously hear us, O Lord.
Lamb of God, who takest away the sins of the world,
Have mercy on us.

Lord have mercy.
Christ have mercy.
Lord have mercy.

Our Father, etc. (secretly)

V. Bless the Lord, all ye his Angels.
R. Ye that are mighty in strength, that fulfil his commandments, hearkening unto the voice of his words.
V. Bless the Lord, all ye his hosts,
R. Ye ministers of his, that do his will.
V. He hath given his Angels charge concerning thee.

LITANY OF THE HOLY ANGELS

R. To keep thee in all thy ways.
V. The Angel of the Lord shall encamp round about them that fear him.
R. And shall deliver them,
V. In the sight of the Angels will I sing unto thee, 0 my God.
R. I will worship toward thy holy temple, and will give praise unto thy name, O Lord,
V. O Lord, hear my prayer.
R. And let my cry come unto thee.

Let us pray.

O God, who dispensest the services of angels and men in a wonderful order; mercifully grant that our life may be protected on earth by those who always do thee service in heaven. Through Jesus Christ our Lord. Amen.

Litany of the Holy Angel Guardian

Lord have mercy.
Lord have mercy.
Christ have mercy.
Christ have mercy.
Lord have mercy.
Lord have mercy.

Christ hear us.
Christ graciously hear us.

God the Father of heaven,
Have mercy on us.
God the Son, Redeemer of the world,
Have mercy on us.
God the Holy Ghost,
Have mercy on us.
Holy Trinity, one God,
Have mercy on

[Respond: *Pray for us.*]
Holy Mary, Queen of Angels,
Holy Angel, my guardian,

Holy Angel, my prince,
Holy Angel, my monitor,
Holy Angel, my counsellor,
Holy Angel, my defender,
Holy Angel, my steward,
Holy Angel, my friend,
Holy Angel, my negotiator,
Holy Angel, my intercessor,
Holy Angel, my patron,
Holy Angel, my director,
Holy Angel, my ruler,
Holy Angel, my protector,
Holy Angel, my comforter,
Holy Angel, my brother,
Holy Angel, my teacher,
Holy Angel, my shepherd,
Holy Angel, my witness,
Holy Angel, my helper,
Holy Angel, my watcher.
Holy Angel, my conductor,
Holy Angel, my preserver,
Holy Angel, my instructor,
Holy Angel, my enlightener,

Lamb of God, who takes away the sins of the world,
Spare us, O Lord.
Lamb of God, who takes away the sins of the world,
Graciously hear us, O Lord.
Lamb of God, who takes away the sins of the world,
Have mercy on us.

Christ hear us,
Christ graciously hear us.

V. Pray for us, O holy Angel-guardian,
R. That we may be made worthy of the promises of Christ.

Let us pray:

Almighty, everlasting God, who, in the counsel of thy ineffable goodness, hast appointed to all the faithful, from their mother's womb, a special Angel-guardian of their body and soul; grant that I may so love and honor him whom thou hast so mercifully given me, that, protected by the bounty of thy grace, and by his assistance, I may merit to behold , with him and all the angelic host, the glory of thy countenance in the heavenly country. Who lives and reigns, world without end. Amen.

Litany of St. Stanislas Kotska

Lord have mercy.
Lord hare mercy,
Christ have mercy.
Christ have mercy.
Lord have mercy.
Lord have mercy.

Christ hear us.
Christ graciously hear us.

[Respond with: *Have mercy on us.*]
God the Father of heaven,
God the Son, Redeemer of sf the world,
God the Holy Ghost,
Holy Trinity, one God,

[Respond with: *Pray for us.*]
Holy Mary,
Holy Mother of God,
Holy Mary, conceived wit out sin,
St. Stanislas Kotska,
Destined to the service of God from thy conception.

Faithful follower of Jesus Christ,
Well-beloved child of Mary,
Called by her to the Company of Jesus,
Faithful to the vocation and grace of God,
Most worthy son of St. Ignatius,
Fair ornament of the Company of Jesus,
Model and patron of novices,
Enemy of the world and of its riches,
Contemner of human glory,
Severe chastiser of thine innocent flesh,
Admirable in thy matchless purity,
Vanquisher of every evil passion,
Exact observer of religious discipline.
Devout adorer of the Sacrament of the Altar,
Treasure of heavenly graces.
Mirror of obedience, humility, and patience,
Model of candour, modesty and piety,
Ardent lover of evangelical poverty,
Wise above thy years,
Lover of brotherly charity,
Penetrated with self-contempt.
Victim of divine love,
Example of Christian youth,
Honoured with the sensible Presence of the Infant Jesus,
An angel in thy life and manners,
Fed by Angels with bread from heaven,
An apostle in zeal and merits,
A martyr in faith and in desire,
A confessor in constant piety,
Ushered into heaven amid a choir of virgins,
Perfect in all virtues, not-withstanding thy short life,

LITANY OF ST. STANISLAS KOTSKA

The ornament and glory of thy ancestors,
The stay and prop of thrones,
The refuge and the safety of all who call upon thee,
Illustrious in the miracles wrought both before and after thy decease.
Most blessed citizen of the heavenly Jerusalem,

Lamb of God, who takest away the sins of the world,
Spare us, O Lord.
Lamb of God, who takest away the sins of the world,
Graciously hear us, O Lord.
Lamb of God, who takest away the sins of the world,
Have mercy on us.

Christ hear us.
Christ graciously hear us.

V. Pray for us, St. Stanislas.
R. That we may be made worthy of the promises of Christ.

Let us pray.

O God, who, amongst other miracles of thy wisdom, hast bestowed even in tender age the grace of matured sanctity; grant, we beseech thee, that, redeeming the time by instant labour, after the example of blessed Stanislas, we may hasten to enter into eternal rest. Through Christ our Lord. Amen.

Litany of St. Vincent de Paul

Lord have mercy.
> *Lord have mercy.*
> Christ have mercy.
> *Christ have mercy.*
> Lord have mercy.
> *Lord have mercy.*

Christ hear us.
> *Christ graciously hear us.*

God the Father of heaven,
> *Have mercy on us.*
> God the Son, Redeemer of the world,
> *Have mercy on us.*
> God the Holy Ghost,
> *Have mercy on us.*
> Holy Trinity, one God,
> *Have mercy on us.*

[Respond: *Pray for us.*]
> Holy Mary,
> St. Vincent of Paul,

St. Vincent, who at the tenderest age didst display a wisdom most mature,

St. Vincent, who, from thy childhood, was full of piety and compassion,

St. Vincent, who, like David, from a simple shepherd became the ruler and pastor of the people of God,

St. Vincent, who in thy captivity didst preserve a perfect freedom,

St. Vincent, the just man, who lived by faith,

St. Vincent, always supported on the firm anchor of a Christian hope,

St. Vincent, always inflamed with the fire of charity,

St. Vincent, truly simple, upright, and fearing God.

St Vincent, true disciple of Jesus Christ, always meek and humble of heart.

St. Vincent, perfectly mortified in heart and mind,

St. Vincent, ever animated with the spirit of Jesus-Christ,

St, Vincent, generous maintainer of the glory of God,

St. Vincent, ever inwardly burning and ever outwardly transported, with zeal for souls,

St. Vincent, who in Christian poverty did find the precious pearl, and the rich g treasure of the Gospel,

St. Vincent, like to the Angels in thy purity,

St. Vincent, ever faithful in obedience, and ever victorious in word,

St. Vincent, from thy earliest years constantly devoted to works of charity.

St. Vincent, who didst fly with most diligent care the slightest appearance of evil,

St. Vincent, who, in all thine actions, didst aspire to the practice of the most perfect virtue,

St. Vincent, who, like a rock, remained immovable amidst the stormy sea of this world,

St. Vincent, who, constant as the sun in its course, went ever onward

in the paths of truest wisdom,
> St. Vincent, always invincible by all the arrows of adversity,
> St Vincent, as patient in suffering as thou was indulgent in forgiving,
> St. Vincent, ever docile and obedient son of the Holy Romain Church,

St. Vincent, who had exceeding horror of the novel ways and subtle words of heresy,
> St. Vincent, destined by a special Providence to announce the Gospel to the poor,
> St. Vincent, tender father and perfect model of ecclesiastics,
> St. Vincent, prudent founder of the Congregation of the Mission,
> St. Vincent, wise institutor of the order Sisters of Charity,
> St. Vincent, always tender in compassion, and always prompt in relieving, all the necessities of the poor,
> St. Vincent, equally fervent in the practice of prayer and in the ministry of the word,
> St. Vincent, perfect imitator of the life and virtues of Jesus Christ,
> St. Vincent, who didst persevere to the end in eschewing evil and doing good,
> St. Vincent, who, as in life so in death, was most precious in the sight of God,

(St. Vincent, who by the knowledge of absolute truth, by the love of sovereign goodness, by the joys of a blessed eternity, possesses perfect happiness,
> *Pray for the members of the Church, and especially for the members of this brotherhood.*)

Lamb of God who takes away the sins of the world,
> *Spare us, O Lord.*

Lamb of God who takes away the sins of the world,
> *Graciously hear us, O Lord.*

LITANY OF ST. VINCENT DE PAUL

Lamb of God who takes away the sins of the world,
Have mercy on us.

V. The Lord had led the just man through right ways.
R. And showed unto him the kingdom of God.

Let us Pray:

Great God, who, by an effect of Thine infinite goodness, has renewed, in our days, in the apostolic charity and humility of thy blessed servant Vincent, the spirit of thy well-beloved Son to preach the Gospel to the poor, relieve the afflicted, console the miserable, and add new luster to the ecclesiastical order; grant, we beseech thee, through his powerful intercession, that we also, being delivered from the great misery of sin, may labor to please thee by the practice of the same humility. Through Jesus Christ our Lord.

Amen.

Litany of Francis Xavier

Lord have mercy.
Lord, have mercy.
Christ, have mercy.
Christ, have mercy.
Lord, have mercy.
Lord, have mercy.

Christ, hear us.
Christ, graciously hear us.

God the Father of heaven,
Have mercy on us.
God the Son, Redeemer of the world,
Have mercy on us.
God the Holy Ghost, Holy Trinity, one God,
Have mercy on us.

[Respond: *Pray for us.*]
   Holy Mary, virgin Mother of God,
   St. Ignatius, founder of the Society of Jesus,
   St. Francis Xavier, the glory of thine order, Apostle of the Indies and Japan,

LITANY OF FRANCIS XAVIER

Legate of the holy Apostolic See Preacher of the truth, and doctor of the nations,
Vessel of election to carry the name of Jesus Christ to the kings of the earth,
Shining light to those who sat in the shadow of death,
Full of zeal for the glory of God,
Unwearied propagator of the Christian faith,
Most watchful shepherd of souls,
Most faithful follower of Jesus Christ,
Most ardent lover of evangelical poverty,
Most perfect observer of religious obedience,
Who didst burn with the fire of divine love,
Who didst generously despise all earthly things,
Most brilliant guide in the way of perfection,
Model of apostolic men,
Model of all virtues,
Light of infidels, and master of the faithful,
Angel in life and manners,
Patriarch in affection and care of God's people,
Prophet mighty in word and works,
Whom all nations and the Church have with one voice associated with the glorious choir of apostles,
Who wast adorned with the crown of virgins,
Who didst aspire to be the palm of martyrs,
Confessor of the faith in word and deed,
Whom the winds and the sea obeyed,
Scourge of demons, arid destroyer of idols,
Powerful defence against shipwreck,
Health of the sick, and salvation of sinners,
Father of the poor, and refuge of the miserable,
Wonderful worker of miracles,

Who wast endowed with the gift of. tongues,
Who wast endowed with the power of raising the dead,
Resounding trumpet of the Holy Ghost,
Light and glory of the East,
[Respond: *We beseech thee, hear us.*]

Through the cross, which thou didst so often raise among the Gentiles,
Through the faith, which thou didst so marvellously propagate,
Through thy miracles and prophecies,
Through the perils and shipwrecks which thou didst endure.
Through thy pains and labors, in the midst of which thou didst so ardently exclaim: Still more, still more!
Through thy heavenly raptures, in the midst of which thou didst so fervently exclaim: Enough, Lord, enough!
Through the glory and happiness which now thou dost enjoy in heaven,

Friend of the heavenly Bridegroom,
Intercede for us.
Blessed Francis Xavier, be loved of God and men,
Intercede for us.

Lamb of God, who takest world, away the sins of the
Spare us, O Lord.
Lamb of God, who takest world, away the sins of the world.
Graciously hear us, O Lord,
Lamb of God, who takest world, away the sins of the
Have mercy on us.

Christ, hear us.
Christ, graciously hear us.

V. Pray for us, St. Francis Xavier.
R. That we may be made worthy of the promises of Christ.

Let us pray.

O God, Who dost glorify those who glorify Thee and Who art honored in the honor which we render to Thy saints; mercifully grant that, in celebrating the glorious memory of the blessed Francis Xavier, we may feel in ourselves the happy effects of his powerful intercession with Thee. Through Our Lord Jesus Christ, Thy Son, Who with Thee and the Holy Ghost, liveth and reigneth world without end. Amen.

V

Other Litanies

A Scriptural Litany

Lord have mercy.
Lord have mercy,
Christ have mercy.
Christ have mercy.
Lord have mercy.
Lord have mercy.

[Respond with: *Have mercy on us.*]
God, the Father of heaven,
God the Son, Redeemer of the world,
God the Holy Ghost,
Holy Trinity, one God,
God, of whom, by whom, and in whom are all things,
God, in whom we live, and move, and are,
Who alone hast immortality, and dwellest in light inaccessible,
Whose majesty filleth the whole earth,
Whom heaven and the heaven of heavens cannot contain,
Who hast made all things for thyself,
Who workest all things according to the counsel of thy will,
In whose hand is the soul of every living thing, and the spirit of all flesh,
Who openest thine hand, and fillest with blessing every living

creature,
> Who hast power to cast body and soul into hell,
> Who dost great things and unsearchable, and wonderful things without number,
> Whose eyes are brighter than the sun, beholding all the ways of men,
> Who catchest the wise in their craftiness, and disappointest the counsel of the wicked,
> Who searchest the heart, and triest the reins,
> Whose judgments are incomprehensible, and whose ways are unsearchable,
> Who art the Father of orphans, and the Judge of widows,
> Merciful and patient, of much compassion, and true,
> Our protector, and our reward exceedingly great,
> King of kings, and Lord of lords,
> King of ages, immortal and invisible,

Be merciful,
> *Spare us, O Lord.*
> Be merciful,
> *Graciously hear us, O Lord.*

[Respond with: *O Lord, deliver us.*]
> From all sin.
> From pride and vain-glory,
> From avarice and worldly solicitude,
> From anger, resentment, and envy,
> From calumny, detraction, and rash judgment,
> From gluttony, drunkenness, and impurity,
> From spiritual sloth, and the forgetfulness of our salvation. From the abuse of thy grace, and a reprobate sense,
> From the worm that never dieth, and the fire that shall never be

extinguished,

From being deprived of the sight and enjoyment of thee, Through thy almighty power and infinite wisdom,

Through thy incomprehensible majesty and eternal glory, Through thy ineffable bounty and superabundant mercy, Through all the humiliations and sufferings of thine only begotten Son,

We sinners,
Beseech thee, hear us.

[Respond with: *We beseech Thee, hear us.*]

That we may love thee, the Lord our God, with all our heart, with all our soul, and with all our mind.

That we may adore thee alone, and serve thee in holiness and righteousness all the days of our lives,

That we may never take thy holy name in vain,

That we may sanctify the feasts and holy days of the Church,

That we may give due honour and obedience to our parents and lawful superiors,

That we may not injure our neighbour in body, soul, or peace of mind,

That we may crucify the flesh, with its vices and concupiscences, and be ever clean of heart,

That we may not do to others what we would not have others do to us,

That we may not covet our neighbour's goods,

That thou wouldst make all grace abound in us.

That we may present our bodies a living sacrifice, holy and acceptable to thee,

That thou wouldst bring us to the kingdom which thou hast prepared for us from the foundation of the world.

Lamb of God, who takest away the sins of the world,
Spare us, O Lord.
Lamb of God, who takest away the sins of the world.
Graciously hear us, O Lord.
Lamb of God, who takest away the sins of the world.
Have mercy on us.

Glory be to the Father, etc.
As it was in the beginning , etc.

Let us pray.

O adorable Lord, in Three distinct and equal Persons One God, who requirest the homage of our reason by the belief of mysteries which are above our understanding, and that of our will by the observance of precepts which are mortifying to our natural inclinations; give us thy grace to perform this two- fold duty, and grant that we may never oppose our uncertain reasoning to thy infallible truth, nor deliberately transgress thy most high and holy commands. Thus continuing until death in entire subjection to thee, may we come at last to the clear and perfect enjoyment of thee. Who livest and reignest world without end. Amen

Litany of the Blessed Sacrament

Lord have mercy on us.
Lord, have mercy on us.
Christ, have mercy on us.
Christ, have mercy on us.
Lord, have mercy on us.
Lord, have mercy on us.

Christ, hear us.
Christ, graciously hear us.

God, the Father of heaven,
Have mercy on us.
God, the Son, Redeemer of the world,
Have mercy on us.
God, the Holy Ghost,
Have mercy on us.
Holy Trinity, one God,
Have mercy on us.

[Respond with: *Have mercy on us.*]
Living Bread, that earnest down from heaven,
Hidden God and Saviour,

Wheat of the elect,
Wine of which virgins are the fruit,
Bread of fatness and royal dainties,
Perpetual sacrifice,
Clean oblation,
Lamb without spot,
Most pure feast,
Food of angels,
Hidden manna,
Memorial of the wonders of God,
Supersubstantial bread,
Word made flesh, dwelling among us,
Sacred Host,
Chalice of benediction,
Mystery of faith,
Most high and most adorable sacrament,
Most holy of all sacrifices,
True propitiation for the living and the dead,
Heavenly antidote against the poison of sin,
Most wonderful of all miracles,
Most holy commemoration of the passion of Christ,
Special memorial of divine love,
Affluence of divine bounty,
Most august and holy mystery,
Medicine of immortality,
Tremendous and life-giving sacrament,
Bread made flesh by the omnipotence of the Word,
Unbloody sacrifice,
Sweetest banquet, at which angels minister,
Sacrament of piety,
Bond of charity,

LITANY OF THE BLESSED SACRAMENT

Priest and victim,
Spiritual sweetness tasted in its proper source;
Refreshment of holy souls,
Viaticum of such as die in the Lord,
Pledge of future glory,

Be merciful
Spare us, O Lord.
Be merciful,
Graciously hear us, O Lord.

[Respond with: *O Lord, deliver us.*]
From an unworthy reception of Thy body and blood,
From the lust of the flesh,
From the lust of the eyes,
From the pride of life,
From every occasion of sin,
Through the desire wherewith Thou didst long to eat this passover with Thy disciples,
Through that profound humility wherewith Thou didst wash their feet,
Through that ardent charity whereby Thou didst institute this divine sacrament,
Through Thy precious blood, which Thou hast left us on our altars,
Through the five wounds of this Thy most holy body, which Thou didst receive for us,

[Respond with: *We beseech thee, hear us.*]
We sinners beseech Thee, hear us.
That Thou wouldst vouchsafe to preserve and increase our faith, reverence, and devotion toward this admirable sacrament,

That Thou wouldst vouchsafe to conduct us, through a true confession of our sins, to a frequent reception of the Holy Eucharist,

That Thou wouldst vouchsafe to deliver us from all heresy, perfidity, and blindness of heart,

That Thou wouldst vouchsafe to impart to us the precious and heavenly fruits of this most holy sacrament,

That at the hour of death Thou wouldst strengthen and defend us by this heavenly viaticum,

Son of God,

Lamb of God, Who takest away the sins of the world,
Spare us, O Lord.
Lamb of God, Who takest away the sins of the world,
Graciously hear us, O Lord.
Lamb of God, Who takest away the sins of the world,
Have mercy on us.
Christ, hear us.
Christ, graciously hear us.

V. Thou didst give them bread from heaven.
R. Containing in itself all sweetness.

Let us pray

O God, Who in this wonderful sacrament has left us a memorial of Thy passion, grant us the grace, we beseech Thee, so to venerate the sacred mysteries of Thy body and blood, that we may constantly experience within ourselves the fruit of Thy redemption. Who livest and reignest forever and ever. Amen.

Litany of the Children of Mary

Lord have mercy on us.
Christ have mercy on us.

Daughter of God the Father, elevated above all creatures, govern
Thy children.
Mother of God the Son, and our Mother, protect
Thy children.
Spouse of the Holy Ghost, obtain the sanctification of
Thy children.

[Respond: *O Mary, hear us!*]
Mother of strength, obtain for thy children the gift of perseverance and courage,
O Mother of love, obtain for thy children a true, generous, and constant love of God,
Mother, full of zeal for the glory of thy Divine Son, obtain for thy children the gift of a g lively, prudent, and enlightened zeal,
Mother, who didst preserve thyself as pure g as the lily in the midst of thorns, obtain for thy children a love of Purity which may preserve them from all sin,
Mother, who didst never lose sight of the presence of God, obtain for thy children the grace ever to remember Him, even amidst the tumults

of this world,

Mother most generous, obtain for thy children patience and resignation in all the trials of this life,

Mother, ever calm, even at the foot of the cross obtain for thy children the spirit of peace, which may sustain us amidst the o afflictions of life,

Mother most faithful, obtain for thy children a lively faith that they may behold God in all his creatures,

Mother most meek and humble, obtain for thy children the virtues of meekness and humility,

Mother, who in all thy actions sought to please thy God, obtain for thy children purity of intention and may our conduct prove as thy true children,

Mother, who didst despise the world and its vanities, obtain for thy children the grace to resist its deceitful charms,

By thy Immaculate Conception, O mother hear thy children!

By the fervor with which thou didst offer thyself to God at the age of three years, O mother hear thy children!

O thou who wert ever resigned to God's holy will, obtain for thy children perfect conformity to the will of God,

O Mother, hear us!

By thy heart pierced with a sword of grief,

O Mother, hear us!

O thou who never forsake those who confide in thee, protect us from the snares of our enemy,

O Mother, hear us!

St. Joseph, faithful guardian of Jesus and Mary,
Pray for us.
Saints Aloysius and Stanislaus, devoted servants of Mary,
Pray for us.

Lamb of God, who takes away the sins of the world,
Hear us, O Lord.
Lamb of God, who takes away the sins of the world,
Spare us, O Lord.
Lamb of God, who takes away the sins of the world.
Have mercy on us.

Jesus, hear us.
Jesus, graciously hear us.

O Mary, full of grace,
Look down upon and bless thy children.

Let us Pray:

O Jesus, who from the cross did give Mary to be the Mother of mankind, and have placed us among her privileged children, grand that, profiting by the graces thou hast so abundantly shed upon us, we may realize the consoling words: "It is impossible that a true servant of Mary should perish." We ask it, O Jesus, by the tenderness of thy divine Heart, and the merits of thy Holy Passion.

Amen.

Litany of the Faithful Departed

Lord, have mercy.
Lord, have mercy.
Christ, have mercy.
Christ, have mercy.
Lord, have mercy.
Lord, have mercy.

Ancient of days, Thy servants meet
   To bow before Thy mercy seat,
   Thou Father, Son, and Paraclete.
   Miserere, Domine.

Have mercy, Lord, on all who wait
   In place forlorn and lonely state,
   Outside Thy peaceful palace gate.
   Miserere, Domine.

These were the work of Thine own bands,
   Thy promise sure forever stands;
   Release them, Lord, from pain and bands.
   Miserere, Domine.

LITANY OF THE FAITHFUL DEPARTED

Lord Jesus, by Thy sacred name,
   By Thy meek suffering and shame,
   Preserve these souls from cruel flame.
Miserere, Domine.

By sweat of blood and crown of thorn,
   By cross to Calvary meekly borne,
   Be Thou to them salvation's horn.
Miserere, Domine.

By Thy five wounds and seven cries,
   By pierced Heart and glazing eyes,
   By Thy dread, awful sacrifice,
Miserere, Domine.

When here below are lifted up
   The sacred Host and blessed cup,
   Soon with Thee, Lord, may each one sup.
Miserere, Domine.

By Raphael's powers and Michael's might,
   By all the ordered ranks of light,
   Battalions of the infinite,
Miserere, Domine.

By martyrs pangs and triumph-palm,
   By saints' strong faith, confessors' psalm,
   By Mary s name, Gilead's balm,
Miserere, Domine.

These souls forlorn, Redeemer blest,
   Never denied Thee, but confest,
   Grant them at last eternal rest.
Miserere, Domine.

On earth they failed from day to day,
   Oft stumbling on the narrow way,
   Yet put their trust in Thee for aye.
Miserere, Domine.

Let their chill desolation cease,
   Thy mercy shed and give release,
   Then grant them everlasting peace.
Miserere, Domine.

Here months and years now come and go,
   With summer gleam and winter snow;
   Let fall Thy dew and grace below.
Miserere, Domine.

Flowers fade and wither; such their doom,
   Men fail and find the gaping tomb:
   With Thee Thy gardens ever bloom.
Miserere, Domine.

Vision of peace so calm and bright,
   After a long and darksome night,
   Clothe them with everlasting light.
Miserere, Domine.

LITANY OF THE FAITHFUL DEPARTED

For these poor souls who may not pray —
   For gone is their probation day —
   We plead Thy cross and humbly say,
Miserere, Domine.

Jesus, for Thee they keenly long,
   To company with saintly throng
   And, ransomed, sing the new glad song.
Miserere, Domine.

May they with saints in glory shine,
   Joined with angelic orders nine;
   Link them with Thee in joys divine.
Miserere, Domine.

Enter may they through heaven's door,
   To walk in white on yonder shore,
   Forever, Lord, for evermore!
Miserere, Domine.

Remember all their sighs and tears,
   One day with Thee a thousand years;
   Give peace, O Lord, and calm their fears!
Miserere, Domine.

As pants the hart for cooling spring,
   As bird flies home with wearied wing,
   Homeward they turn, Lord, homeward bring.
Miserere, Domine.

Let us pray

Ye souls of the faithful, who sleep in the Lord,
   But as yet are shut out from your final reward!
   Oh! would I could lend you assistance to fly
   From your prison below, to your palace on high!

O Father of mercies! Thine anger withhold;
   These works of Thine hand In Thy mercy behold;
   Too oft from Thy path they have wandered aside;
   But Thee, their creator they never denied.

O tender Redeemer! Their misery see;
   Deliver the souls that were ransomed by Thee;
   Behold how they love Thee, despite of their pain;
   Restore them, restore them to favor again.

O spirit of grace! O Consoler divine!
   See how for Thy presence they longingly pine;
   Ah then, to enliven their sadness, descend!
   And fill them with peace, and with joy in the end.

O Mother of mercy! Dear Mother in' grief!
   Lend thou to their torments a balmy relief;
   Attemper the rigor of justice severe;
   And soften their flame with a pitying tear.

Ye patrons! who watched o'er their safety below;
   Oh! think how they need your fidelity now;
   And stir all the angels and saints of the sky
   To plead for the souls that upon you rely.

LITANY OF THE FAITHFUL DEPARTED

Ye friends, who once sharing their pleasures and pain,
  Now haply already in paradise reign!
  Oh, comfort their hearts With a whisper of love;
  And call them to share in your pleasures above!

O fountain of goodness! Accept our sighs;
  Let Thy mercy bestow what Thy justice denies;
  So may Thy poor captives, released from their woes,
  Thy praises proclaim while eternity flows.

All ye, who would honor the saints and their Head,
  Remember, remember, to pray for the dead;
  And they, in return, from their misery freed,
  To you will be friends in the hour of need.
  Amen.

Litany for a Happy Death

Lord, have mercy on us.
Lord, have mercy on us.
Christ, have mercy on us.
Christ, have mercy on us.
Lord, have mercy on us.
Lord, have mercy on us.

Christ, hear us.
Christ, graciously hear us.

God, the Father of heaven.
Have mercy on us.
God, the Son, Redeemer of the world.
Have mercy on us.
God, the Holy Ghost.
Have mercy on us.
Holy Trinity, one God.
Have mercy on us.

[Respond with: *Pray for us.*]
Holy Mary,
All ye holy angels and archangels,

Holy Abraham,
St. John the Baptist,
St. Joseph,
All ye holy patriarchs and prophets,
St. Peter,
St. Paul,
St. Andrew,
St. John,
St. Jude,
All ye holy apostles and evangelists,
All ye holy disciples of Our Lord,
All ye holy innocents,
St. Stephen,
St. Lawrence,
All ye holy martyrs,
St. Sylvester,
St. Gregory,
St. Augustine,
St. Basil,
St. Ambrose,
St. Francis de Sales,
St. Vincent de Paul,
St. Aloysius,
St. Stanislaus,
All ye holy bishops and confessors,
St. Benedict,
St. Dominic,
St. Francis of Assisi,
St. Ignatius,
St.. Philip Neri,
St. Camillus de Lellis,

St. John of God,
All ye holy monks, hermits, and founders of Religious Orders,
St. Mary Magdalen,
St. Lucy,
St. Scholastica,
St. Teresa,
St. Catharine,
St. Clara,
St. Ursula,
St. Angela Merici,
St. Jane Frances de Chantal,
St. Barbara,
All ye holy virgins and widows,
All ye saints of God, intercede for us.

Be merciful unto us.
Spare us, O Lord.
Be merciful unto us.
Hear us, O Lord.

[Respond with: *O Lord, deliver us.*]
From Thine anger,
From an evil death,
From the pains of hell,
From all evil,
From the power of the devil,
By Thy nativity,
By Thy cross and passion,
By Thy death and burial,
By Thy glorious resurrection,
By the grace of the Holy Ghost the Comforter,

LITANY FOR A HAPPY DEATH

In the day of judgment,
We sinners, beseech Thee, hear us.

[Respond with: *We beseech Thee, hear us.*]
That Thou wouldst spare us,
That Thou wouldst vouchsafe to bring us unto true repentance,
That Thou wouldst vouchsafe to grant eternal rest to all the faithful departed,

Lamb of God, Who takest away the sins of the world,
Spare us, O Lord.
Lamb of God, Who takes away the sins of the world,
Graciously hear us, O Lord.
Lamb of God, Who takest away the sins of the world,
Have mercy on us.

Lord, have mercy on us.
Christ, have mercy on us.
Lord, have mercy on us.

V. We adore Thee, O Christ, and we bless Thee.
R. Because by Thy holy cross Thou hast redeemed the world.

Let us pray

Divine Jesus, incarnate Son of God, Who for our salvation didst vouchsafe to be born in a stable, to pass Thy life in poverty, trials, and misery, and to die amid the sufferings of the cross, I entreat Thee in the hour of my death, say to Thy divine Father: "Father, forgive him;" say to Thy beloved Mother: "Behold thy son;" say to my soul: "This day thou shalt be with me in paradise." My God, my God, forsake me not in that hour. "I thirst;" truly, my God, my soul thirsts after Thee, Who art the fountain of living waters. My life passes like a shadow; yet a little while and all will be consummated. Wherefore, O my adorable Saviour, from this moment, for all eternity, "Into Thy hands I commend my spirit." Lord Jesus, receive my soul. Amen.

Litany for Holy Communion

(For before or after Holy Communion)

Lord, have mercy on us.
    Christ, have mercy on us.
    Lord, have mercy on us.
    Christ, hear us.
    Christ, graciously hear us.

[Respond with: *Have mercy on us.*]
    God, the Father of heaven,
    God, the Son, redeemer of the world,
    God, the Holy Ghost,
    Holy Trinity, one God,
    Jesus, living bread which came down from heaven,
    Jesus, bread from heaven giving life to the world,
    Hidden God and Saviour,
    My Lord and my God, Who hast loved us with an everlasting love,
    Whose delights are to be with the children of men,
    Who hast given Thy flesh for the life of the world,
    Who dost invite all to come to Thee,
    Who dost promise eternal life to those who receive Thee,
    Who with desire dost desire to eat this Pasch with us,

Who art ever ready to receive and welcome us,
Who dost stand at our door knocking,
Who hast said that if we will open to Thee the door, Thou wilt come in and sup with us,
Who dost receive us into Thy arms and bless us with the little children,
Who dost suffer us to sit at Thy feet with Magdalen,
Who dost invite us to lean on Thy bosom with the beloved disciple,
Who hast not left us Most orphans,
Most dear sacrament,
Sacrament of love,
Sacrament of sweetness,
Life-giving sacrament,
Sacrament of strength,
My God, and my all.

[Respond with: *We beseech Thee, hear us.*]

That our hearts may pant after Thee as the hart after the fountains of water,
That Thou wouldst manifest Thyself to us as to the two disciples in the breaking of bread,
That we may know Thy voice like Magdalen,
That with a lively faith we may confess with the beloved disciple — "It That is the Thou Lord,"
That Thou wouldst bless us who have not seen and have believed,
That we may love Thee in the Blessed Sacrament with our whole heart, with our whole soul, with all our mind, and with all our strength,
That the fruit of each communion may be fresh love,
That our one desire may be to love Thee and to do Thy will,
That we may ever remain in Thy love,
That Thou wouldst teach us how to receive and welcome Thee,

That Thou wouldst teach us to pray, and Thyself pray within us,
That with Thee every virtue may come into our souls,
That through this day Thou wouldst keep us closely united to Thee,
That Thou wouldst give us grace to persevere to the end,
That Thou wouldst then be our support and Viaticum,
That with Thee and leaning on Thee we may safely pass through all dangers,
That our last act may be one of perfect love, and our last breath a long deep sigh to be in our Father's house,
That Thy sweet face may smile upon us when we appear before Thee,
That our banishment from Thee, dearest Lord, may not be very long,
That when the time is come, we may fly up from our prison to Thee and in Thy sacred Heart find our rest forever,

Lamb of God, Who takest away the sins of the world,
Spare us, O Lord.
Lamb of God, Who takest away the sins of the world,
Graciously hear us.
Lamb of God, Who takest away the sins of the world,
Have mercy on us.

V. Stay with us, Lord because it is toward evening.
R. And the day is now far spent.

Let us pray

We come to Thee, dear Lord, with the apostles, saying, "Increase our faith." Give us a strong and lively faith in the mystery of Thy real presence in the midst of us. Give us the splendid faith of the centurion, which drew from Thee such praise. Give us the faith of the beloved disciple, to know Thee in the dark and say, "It is the Lord!" Give as the faith of Martha to confess, "Thou art Christ the Son of the living God." Give us the faith of Magdalen to fall at Thy feet crying, "Rabboni, Master." Give us the faith of all Thy saints, to whom the Blessed Sacrament has been heaven begun on earth. In every communion increase our faith; for with faith love and humility, and reverence and all good, will come into our souls. Dearest Lord, *increase our faith*. Amen.

Litany of the Holy Cross

Lord have mercy.
Lord have mercy.
Christ have mercy.
Christ have mercy.
Lord have mercy.
Lord have mercy.

Christ hear us.
Christ graciously hear us.

[Respond with: *Have mercy on us.*]
   God the Father of heaven,
   God the Son, Redeemer of the world,
   God the Holy Ghost,
   Holy Trinity, one God,

Holy Cross, whereon the Lamb of God was offered for the sins of the world,
   Deliver and save us.

[Respond with: *Save us, O Holy Cross.*]
   Hope of Christians,

Pledge of the resurrection from the dead,
Shelter of persecuted innocence,
Guide of the blind,
Way of those who have gone astray,
Staff of the lame,
Consolation of the poor,
Restraint of the powerful,
Destruction of the proud,
Reguse of sinners,
Trophy of victory over hell,
Terror of demons,
Mistress of youth,
Succour of the distressed,
Hope of the hopeless,
Star of the mariner,
Harbour of the wrecked,
Rampart of the besieged,
Father of orphans,
Defence of widows,
Counsel of the just,
Judge of the wicked,
Rest of the afflicted,
Safeguard of childhood,
Strength of manhood,
Last nope of the aged,
Light of those who sit in darkness,
Splendour of kings,
Civilizer of the world,
Buckler impenetrable,
Wisdom of the foolish,
Liberty of slaves,

Knowledge of the ignorant,
Sure rule of life,
Heralded by prophets,
Preached by apostles,
Glory of martyrs,
Study of anchorites,
Chastity of virgins,
Joy of priests,
Foundation of the Church,
Salvation of the world.
Destruction of idolatry.
Stumbling-block of the Jews,
Condemnation of the ungodly,
Support of the weak.
Medicine of the sick,
Health of the leprous.
Strength of the paralytic.
Bread of the hungry.
Fountain of those that thirst.
Clothing of the naked.

Lamb of God, who wast offered on the cross for the sins of the world.
Spare us, O Lord.
Lamb of God, who wast offered on the cross for the sins of the world,
Graciously hear us, O Lord.
Lamb of God, who wast offered on the cross for the sins of the world,
Have mercy on us.

Lord hare mercy.
   Christ have mercy.
   Lord have mercy.

V. We adore thee, O Christ, and we bless thee.
R. Because through thy holy Cross thou hast redeemed the world.

Let us pray.

O God, who, for the redemption of the world, wast pleased to be born in a stable, and to die upon a cross; O Lord Jesus Christ, by thy holy Sufferings, which we, thy unworthy servants, devoutly call to mind, by thy holy Cross, and by thy Death, deliver us from the pains of hell, and vouchsafe to conduct us whither thou didst conduct the thief who was crucified with thee. Who livest and reignest eternally in heaven. Amen.

Litany of Penance

Lord have mercy.
Lord have mercy.
Christ have mercy.
Christ have mercy.
Lord have mercy.
Lord have mercy.

Christ hear us.
Christ graciously hear us.

[Respond with: Have mercy on us.]
God the Father of heaven,
God the Son, Redeemer of the world,
God the Holy Ghost,
Holy Trinity, one God,
God of all goodness, who wiliest not the death of a sinner, but rather that & he should be converted g and live,
Who pardonedst not the Angels that sinned, but cast them down to hell for all eternity,
Who, when Adam fell, didst call him to confession and repentance for his sin,
Who didst preserve Noah from the flood, and from the lot of the

ungodly, by saving him in the ark,
Who didst draw Lot from the midst of sinners.
Who, softened by the prayers of Moses, didst forgive the sins of the backsliding people.
Who didst pardon the sin of David, after his confession and repentance,
Who didst spare Achab when he humbled himself in penance,
Who didst graciously hear the penitent Manasses and establish him on his throne,
Who didst grant pardon to the Ninevites, when they did penance for their sins in fasting, and in sack-cloth and ashes,
Who didst succour the Machabees, when they fasted and lay in ashes.
Who didst command thy priests to weep, and pray, and offer sacrifice for the people
Who didst come into the world to save sinners,
Who, when thou wouldst redeem the world, didst send as thy messenger John the Baptist, the preacher of penance.
Who didst fast forty days and forty nights,
Who didst prevent, with thy grace, Matthew, sitting at the receipt of custom,
Who didst bear witness that the Publican, humbly striking his breast, was justified,
Who didst deliver the paraalytic from his infirmity, when thou hadst forgiven him his sins,
Who, by the example of the Prodigal son, didst offer to sinners the hope of pardon,
Who didst make known to the woman of Samaria the fountain of living water.
Who didst bring salvation to the house of Zacheus, repenting of his sins, and making restitution fourfold,
Who didst exercise thy mercy in behalf of the woman taken in

adultery,
> Who didst receive publicans and sinners, and didst eat with them,
> Who didst forgive Magdalen her many sins, because she loved much,
> Who, looking tenderly on Peter, who denied thee,
> didst bring him to compunction and to tears.
> Who didst promise Paradise to the penitent thief.
> Who lovest all thy creatures, and hatest nothing that thou hast made,
> Who givest to sinners both place and time for repentance,
> Who didst come to seek and to save that which was lost,
> Who hast pity on all men, and hidest the sins of those who truly repent,
> Who wouldst have mercy, and not sacrifice.
> Who, when we repent, rememberest our sins no more,
> God, most merciful and patient, tender and loving- kind, notwithstanding all our sins.

We sinners.
Beseech thee, hear us.

[Respond with: *We beseech Thee, hear us.*]
> That thou wouldst vouchsafe to lead us to a true repentance.
> That we may judge ourselves, and so escape thy judgment.
> That we may bring forth in due time worthy fruits of penance.
> That, denying ungodliness and worldly desires, we may live soberly, justly, and godly.
> That sin may not reign in our mortal body.
> That we may not love the world, nor the things of the world.
> That we may work out our salvation with fear and trembling.
> Son of God,

Lamb of God, who takest away the sins of the world,
> *Spare us, O Lord.*
> Lamb of God, who takest away the sins of the world,
> *Graciously hear us, O Lord.*
> Lamb of God, who takest away the sins of the world,
> *Have mercy on us.*

Christ hear us.
> *Christ graciously hear us.*

V. O Lord, hear our prayer.
> **R**. And let our cry come unto thee.

Let us pray.

O most gracious and most merciful God, look with compassion on the frailty of our mortal nature, and sustain our endeavours by thy grace, that, through thy boundless mercy, we may obtain the pardon of nil our sins, persevere constantly in thy service, and in the end attain unto everlasting life. Through Jesus Christ our Lord. Amen,

The Golden Litany

Lord hare mercy on us,
 Christ have mercy on us; and grant us strength of soul, inward and outward, that we may serve thee to the pleasure of thy will.

[Respond with: *Have mercy on us.*]
 O Lord God, Father of heaven, by thy heavenly virtue,
 O Son of God, Redeemer of the world,
 O Holy Ghost, one God, with the Father and the Son,
 O Lord God, by thine increate and undivided Trinity,
 By thy godly being,
 By thy godly nature,
 By thine infinite beauty,
 By thyself, and all goodness that thou beholdest in thyself
 By the creation of heaven and earthy and all things that are in them.
 By thy goodness, which thou hadst in the creation of man to thine image and likeness.
 By that great love, wherewith thou didst predestinate to repair fallen man,
 By that ineffable love, whereby thou chosest Mary, most pure virgin, to be thy mother,
 By that most holy name, Mary, which descended and flowed from the high throne of the glorious Trinity,

By the Immaculate Conception of thy blessed Virgin Mother,
By her most holy Nativity,
By her virginity and great meekness,
By that meek affection and love which drew thee from the bosom of the Father into the womb of the Virgin,
By the humility of thy high majesty, which disdained not to descend into the womb of the Virgin Mary,
For the frailty of man, which thou loathedst not to take willingly for our sins,
For thy holy Nativity, wherein thou didst vouchsafe to be born of a woman,
For that unspeakable delight and gladness, which thy blessed Mother had in thy Nativity,
By that cold crib thou layeat in, wrapped in poor clothes and fed with maiden's milk.
By the great joy of the shepherds, who worshipped thee lying in the crib,
For that painful Circumcision and shedding of thy precious blood, and for the virtue of thy Holy Name Jesus, and all thy blessed names,
For the oblation and the prayers of the three kings,
For that blessed oblation, wherein thou wert offered to thy Father in the temple.
For thy flight into Egypt, and all the pains thou suffe edst there with thy blessed Mother,
For thy coming again from Egypt unto Nazareth, and thy meek obedience wherewith thou didst willingly subject thyself to thy parents,
For thy meek and lowly conversation during three and thirty years on earth,
For thy meek obedience and great patience.
For thy most holy meditations, words, and works of mercy.
For thy holy Baptism, and the glorious appearing of the Holy Trinity,

For thy holy fasting, contemplation, genuflexions, and the tempting of the devil in the desert.

For thy thirst, hunger, cold, and heat, which thou sufferedst in this vale of misery

For thy heaviness, labour, and weariness.

For the detraction and evil words, wherewith thy enemies reviled thee,

For thy watching and prayers.

For thy wholesome doctrine and benefits, and thy mighty resistance, whereby thou gavest no place to thine enemies.

For the wonderful signs and miracles thou wroughtest.

For thy meek and holy conversation.

For thy holy tears, and meek enthronisation in Jerusalem on the day of palms,

For that cursed council, wherein the malicious conspired thy death,

By that fervent and charitable desire that thou hadst to redeem us,

By that great lowliness, which thou shewedst in washing the feet of thy disciples, and of Judas, who betrayed thee,

For thy most noble and worthy institution of the sacrament of thy most precious Body and Blood,

For that profound love, whereby thou sufferedst St. John the Evangelist to rest upon thy breast at supper,

For peace which thou gavest to thy disciples,

For thy holy words and sermons,

For the inward and great heaviness which thou hadst, when thou prayedst to thy Father in the garden beside the Mount of Olivet,

By the virtue of thy holy prayer, that thou prayedst there three times.

For thy fearful dread of thy death,

For that Agony wherein thou offeredst thyself willingly to death, obeying thy Almighty Father, and for thy Bloody Sweat,

By thy great meekness, wherewith thou didst vouchsafe to be

comforted by an angel, so comfort me in every time; and

By thy mighty and victorious courage, wherewith thou wentest to meet them that sought thee to the death,

For thy great goodness, in that thou refusedst not the kiss of Judas, thy betrayer; and the ear of Malchus, that Peter smote off, thou didst restore and heal.

For those holy bonds, that thou wert bound with, and led as a prisoner, and the opprobrious words that thou sufferedst all that night.

For the buffet thou enduredst in the presence of the high priest Annas, and other shame done to thee.

For that love and charity that thou hadst, when thou wert brought bound before the high priest Caiphas,

By the false witnesses ; brought against thee and thy unrighteous condemnation,

By the spitting on thee, and the scourging of thee.

By the buffets and sore strokes given to thee,

By the binding and blind-folding of thy holy eyes, shames and reproaches, that thou sufferedst all that night,

For that merciful look wherewith thou beheldest Peter, and for all that labour and torment, secret and unknown, which thou sufferedst all that night,

By thy presentation before Pilate, and the accusations that the Jews made against thee,

For the contempt and 3 mocking that thou sufferedst of Herod, and the white garment that he sent thee in again to Pilate,

For all the shames, labours, upbraidings, and reproofs, which thou sufferedst going from one judge to another,

For thy great patience and stillness,

For the shameful stripping of thy clothes, and the binding of thy most holy body to a pillar,

For thy scourgings and cruel beatings,

For thy innumerable wounds, and the plenteous shedding of thy blood.

For all thy pain, sorrow, cold, and trembling,

For thy purple garments,

and thy crown of thorns violently pressed upon thy head.

For the grievous pain that thou sufferedst in thy head, crowned with thorns, when it was smitten with the reed.

By the scornful worshipping of the Jews, and their salutation, when they said: Hail, King of the Jews,

By the spitting on thy godly face, and cruel beatings,

For that heaviness of heart, which thou hadst when Pilate brought thee before the multitude of the people, wearing the crown of thorns and the purple vesture, and said to them. Behold the man,

For that fearful sentence of death and shameful leading to the Mount of Calvary,

For thy great love shewed to us, when thou bearedst thy heavy cross upon thy shoulders, to the place where thou sufferedst thy most painful passion; and the labour, anguish, slanders, and beatings that thou sufferedst by the way,

For all thy bloody steps, that thou madest going to thy death.

By the great weariness that thou hadst in thy shoulders, bearing the cross, until thou fellest down.

By the great compassion of thy heart, that thou hadst when, bearing the cross, thou mettest thy blessed Mother sorrowing and making lamentation,

By fhy heaviness of soul and the going up the Mount of Calvary, where thou wert crucified,

By the stripping of thy clothes to thy great shame, in the sight of thy blessed Mother and all the people,

By that cold sitting, wherein thou sattest piteously, full of wounds, in the cold winds, so abiding until thy cross was ready,

For those sore and painful steps thou madest going to thy cross,

For thy great anguish, mournings, and weepings,

For the great stretching of thy sinews and veins, and all thy members,

By the nailing of thy right hand and shedding of thy precious blood, cleanse us, Lord, from all sin, and

By the nailing of thy left hand, and thy most holy wound and precious blood, save and,

For the nailing of thy most holy feet, and by the wounds in them, and the precious blood flowing out of them,

Purge us, enlighten us, and reconcile us to God the Father, and

For the lifting up of thy most holy body on the cross, and thy sore bruising thereof, that gave to all parts of thy body an incredible pain,

For the heaviness of thy heart, and all the powers of thy soul, save us, deliver us, and

For the parting of thy clothes, and the lot that they cast upon thy coat, that was made without seam, thou beholding it,

For thy great love, whereby thou didst hang alive upon the cross three hours,

For the opprobrious and scornful words, which, hanging on the cross, thou heardest spoken to thee,

For the blaspheming, sorrow, and confusion, which thou sufferedst on the cross,

For all the sorrow and pain that thou sufferedst in thy ribs, reins, and shoulders, in time of thy crucifying,

For all the pain thou sufferedst in thy hands and feet, and the straining of all thy members on the cross,

For that wonderful charity, wherewith thou prayedst thy Almighty Father for thine enemies,

For thy great mercy, wherewith thou promisedst paradise to the thief hanging on thy right side,

For the tender care that thou hadst for thy Mother in thy torments, commending her to thy well beloved disciple John,

For that great and miserable cry that thou madest to thy Father,

For the sword of sorrow that went through the soul of thy blessed Mother, and her great compassion and tears, that, standing by the cross, lamentably she shed,

For those holy tears that thou sheddest on the cross, and in all thy life-time,

For thy thirst and tasting of gall and vinegar, grant us to taste the sweetness of thy spirit, and

For all those holy words that thou spakest on the cross, and in all thy life,

For that piteous cry, in the which thou commendedst thy soul to thy Father, our souls be commended to thee; and

By the departing of thy holy soul from thy blessed godly body,

By the resting of thy most s blessed head upon thy breast, incline, most sweet Jesus, to us; and

By the bitterness of thy death, and the intolerable pains wherewith thy heart brake.

By the opening of thy side with a spear, and the flowing out of thy most precious blood, smite through, good Lord, my heart with the spear of thy godly love; and

By that precious blood and water that ran out of thy most holy heart, wash and cleanse us in the same most holy water and blood from all our sins; and

For that great mercy that thou shewedst to Longinus the soldier, and to the centurion; and all thy mercies that thou hast ever shewed to man,

By the descending of thy holy soul to hell,

By that might and strength of thy blessed soul, whereby thou brakest the gates of hell, and deliveredst the souls of thy friends,

For the taking down of thy most holy body from the cross, and the solemn burying thereof; and great lamentation of thy blessed Mother,

Mary Magdalene, and others, thy friends,

For all thy painful labours, weariness, sorrow, and heaviness, which thou sufferedst from the day of thy Nativity unto the hour that thy soul departed from thy body,

For thy glorious Resurrection in body and soul,

For that ineffable joy and gladness of thy blessed Mother, and others, thy friends, in thy glorious Resurrection,

For that special grace, when thou appear east in a glorious body, after thy Resurrection, to Mary Magdalene, to other women, and to thy disciples.

For thy wonderful and glorious Ascension, comfort us, good Lord, in all necessities; and

For thy godly and comfortable sending of the Holy Ghost to thy disciples, comfort us, hallow us, strengthen us in faith, hope, and charity ; and

For thy glory, and the divine majesty and virtues of thy Holy Name, save us and govern us now and ever; and

For the love that rested both in thy Godhead and manhood,

For that joy whereby thou hast fruition in thyself,

For thyself and all goodness and merits that thou a beholdest both in thee, and in thy blessed Mother,

For the ministering of St. Michael, and my good angel deputed for my keeping, and all other spirits of heaven,

By the intercession and merits of SS. Peter and Paul, St. John Evangelist, and all the apostles,

By the merits and intercession of thy holy martyrs,

Laurence, Stephen, and all others,

By the merits and prayers of the holy fathers and confessors, Austin, Anthony, and all others,

By the merits and prayers of Sts. Anne, Catherine, Barbara, and all other holy virgins, widows, and chaste lives.

By the merits and prayers of all thy chosen saints, which are, have been, and are to come in heaven and in earth.

Succour us, most sweet Jesus, in that fearful day of the strict judgment; and grant us in this transitory life all things necessary to the health of body and soul; and after this life, to live and rejoice with thee everlastingly. Amen.

Bibliography

The litanies in this book were compiled from the following traditional sources. These works are all in the public domain.

Catholic Hours, or the Family Prayer Book of all Public and Private Devotions. London: R. Washbourne, 1868.

The Golden Manual: Being a Guide to Catholic Devotion, Public and Private. London: Burns and Lambert, 1850.

The Manual of the Sacred Heart: A Select Volume of Prayer for Daily Use. London: Burns, Lambert, and Oates, 1866.

Lasance, Francis Xavier. *The Blessed Sacrament Book.* New York: Benziger Brothers, 1918.

Lasance, Francis Xavier. *With God: A Book of Prayers and Reflections.* New York: Benziger Brothers, 1911.

Printed in Great Britain
by Amazon